D1737132

The LOGOS Concept

in John's Gospel

&

Correlations with

Science

Teodor Dumitru

A Graded Thesis for the Degree of

Doctor of Philosophy In Biblical Studies

September 2023

Abstract

The *Logos* concept has a major importance in theology, philosophy and sciences. The main motivation for this dissertation is the first verse in John's Gospel: 'In the beginning was the *Word* (Gr. Logos)'. *Logos* had more meanings, as (1) a designer's *expressed thinking* leading to the creation of a system, and *logos* as (2) a system *descriptor* (*system logos*), containing the *designs* (*form* in Greek thinking) of its components plus their *logical relations*. A *logos* from the designer's *expressed thinking* and the *system logos* that corresponds to it are similar in essence. The Universe Designer's *expressed thinking* was considered the *Universe Logos*. **The first part** is a study about the concepts of *Word of God* and *Wisdom* from Old Testament as a possible precursor of the *Logos* concept, about the development of the concept by Greek thinkers, and about the presentation of Lord Jesus as *Logos* by apostles and Christian apologists, to assert His Deity. We study the *Logos concept* with the goal of making it accessible in layman terms and to prepare for our discussion about *logos* and science. **In the second part**, we present how *logos* correlates with contemporary science that put emphasis on *information* and *relations,* mostly in biology and physics. Also in software, Object Oriented Modeling uses *forms (as classes[1]) & their relations,* thus supporting the *logos* culture.

Logos has a *personal* aspect, through the designer, and an *informational aspect*, through the system description. We suggest that the *informational aspect* could be discussed with *information science terms*. We also suggest based on software design, that for any systems' design (man-made or natural) *logos is essential.* This observation corresponds with John's statement *'all things were made through Logos'.*

---

[1] *Class* is code that describes an object, for example a Dog class, from which more Dog objects can be put on screen. They can be considered as the *forms* of Greek thought.

Contents

I. INTRODUCTION

The Gospel of John brings Lord Jesus Christ to our attention from an eternal perspective, in the first verse:

"In the beginning (Gr. *arche*) was the Word (Gr. *Logos*)". (John 1:1 NKJV)[2]

The Greek word *'logos'* has been translated as *'word'*, but in the Greek culture of those times, *'logos'* had a broader meaning, which we will study to understand better John's first chapter, where it is used multiple times; also, we will analyze the possible backgrounds of John's statements.[3] Such a study is important, as in the beginning, or *essence* (Gr. arche) of everything is *Logos*. A good understanding, expressed in common language as we intend, would help Christians to clarify their faith in God and the deity of Christ, as they did in early church. We believe this study is also important because of our claim that some *informational* aspects of *Logos* could

---

[2] All Bible texts from NKJV, through biblegateway.com
[3] Self-citation, also for more places where I get ideas from my work (T. Dumitru, Logos as Expressed Thinking)

have a better explanation through *information* science concepts.

John declares that the primordial essence (Gr. *arche,* in wider meaning) of the world is spiritual, not material. Also, John writes in the same Gospel that *'Logos'* is our Lord Jesus:

> And the Word became flesh and dwelt among us, and we beheld His glory, the glory as of the only begotten of the Father, full of grace and truth. (John 1:14)

Logos became man to bring us graceful forgiveness and true justification. We thank the Lord that He became like us to take away 'the sins of the world' (John 1:29).

A. Purpose

This dissertation has two related parts, both dealing with the concept of *Logos.*

In Part One, we study the concept before Christ, in New Testament, and short after Christ. We emphasize that (1) the concepts of Word of God and Wisdom from Old Testament may be *precursors* of the *Logos* concept, that (2) Apostle John *elevated* the meaning of *Logos* by connecting it to Lord Jesus Christ, and that (3) *Logos* was a *principal* concept employed by theologians to sustain the Deity of Lord Jesus, in the beginning of Christianity, and we should follow them.

In Part Two, we claim that using the concept of *Logos* in contemporary science, one can show that the material and spiritual world is the result of the *expressed thinking* of the *Main Designer*, as John says: "All things were made through Him (*Logos*)." (John 1:3) Then, we claim that *information* science can add justifications for the *informational* aspect of *Logos,* and could explain it in a more appropriate manner.

1. About Part One: Logos before Christ and early Christianity

We analyze the concept of *Logos,* how it is used in Apostle John's time and how he was influenced by Jewish and Greek cultures. Apostle Paul too uses aspects of the *Logos* concept, without stating the term.

We look for concepts that seem like the *Logos* concept in the Old Testament, then study several Greek thinkers which refer to *Logos* and some Jewish writers before Christ; then, we analyze the Apostles John and Paul and early theologians who explained the Deity of Lord Jesus through *Logos*.

From these sources, we focus on the most important meanings of *logos:*

- *a designer's expressed thinking* leading to the creation of a system
- or *logos as* a system *descriptor* (we call it *system logos*), containing the *designs* of its components plus their *logical relations.*

A specific *logos in the thoughts of a designer* and the *logos of a system* that corresponds to it are similar in essence. Also, *all logos*-es in the *Universe Designer's thoughts* and the *system logos*-es corresponding to them are similar in essence. The *Universe Designer's expressed thinking* was considered the *Logos of the Universe.*

In the above meanings of Logos, the meanings of secondary terms are, shortly:

- *Designer* refers to a human who makes projects of systems, or, in these sources also to the highest layer of *Logos*, the conscious Being who designed and created with unifying purpose all layers of systems in Universe (atoms to galaxies, souls, moral code, etc.).

- *Expressed thinking* refers to a thought that is expressed, and eventually implemented in material entities, or describes a system.

- For the *creation* or *description of a system* (with *components and their relations*), it may be that there are two or more *designers or persons* which have a *dialogue* about it. The e*xpressed thinking* of two persons make-up a *dialogue*. Thus, the logical exchange of *expressed thoughts, the dia-logue* (Gr. through logos), is also a kind of *logos.*

- *The Design* (project) of a component refers to the characteristics of each component of a system. It relates to the word *form*[4] in early Greek thinking (explained further).

- *Logical relations* refer to the bindings between the components of a system, to make it useful. They are *logical*, not random[5], as they are the result of *thinking*. They can be bi-directional (or multi).

---

[4] *Form* in Greek thought represented all the characteristics of an object, while in usual English, it is only the exterior format.
[5] Besides logical relations, there are random relations too, as the wind blowing leaves.

Details about Forms, Relations and Logos

As a *system logos* contains *forms (designs) & their relations*, we need to explain first what *form* means.

a. Forms as designs

The concept of *form* (Gr. morphe) was proposed by Plato (4th century B.C.) [6]. For him, every concrete *object* is fabricated from an abstract entity named *form*, as a house is fabricated from a *design* and, similarly we say, a software *object* (like a dog on screen) is fabricated from a design captured in *class* code. A *class* is code that describes the attributes & functions of an *object*; for example, a *Dog class* is code from which more *Dog objects* can be put on screen. A *class* is the *form* of a software *object*. As *forms* with their *relations* are parts of *Logos*, we note that *Logos* has a *personal* aspect, through the designer, and an *informational* aspect, through the system

---

[6] Details and citations in 'Plato' chapter. Here only definitions.

description. We suggest that the informational aspect could be discussed with information science terms.

An important note: An *idea* of a *form* represents the designer's *purpose*, in Greek thought.

The words *kind, type, class, or genre* (Gr. *genos*) relate to the concept of *form* (Coxon, 3).

In Genesis, there are statements about *kinds* (similar with *forms*), by which Elohim brought into existence *objects* of plants and animals, each of their *kind (as form or design)*. Philo of Alexandria (1st century), clarifies that Genesis established the concept of *form / kind* much before Greek thinkers[7].

b. Logical Relations between Forms

Forms can have multiple types of *logical relations* and these are essential in the design of systems from sub-systems as components. We describe these types in 'Plato' chapter.

---

[7] Details and citations in 'Philo' chapter. Here only definitions.

A *logical relation* can be made of one or multiple bi-directional *links* (physical, chemical etc.) or made of an exchange of *messages,* in a *logical sequence.*

A *link* example: in a plant, the Leaf *form* has *logical relations* with the Stem *form*, which has *logical relations* with the Flower *form*. Those three *forms* with their *logical relations* make up the Plant *logos,* which becomes a real-life *system*.

A *message* example: the dialogue (from Gr. dia-logos, through-logos) between two persons to make up a company, as a system, is the *logical relation* that leads to the *company logos.*

Forms can *associate* in a higher-level *form*, as in the plant example.

A *form* can *inherit* characteristics from a higher-level *form*, as Cat *form inherits* from Animal *form*. Instead of *inherit*, we can say that a form *derives* from another form.

The terms *form* as *class*[8], *logical relations, association, inheritance, derivation*, are also used similarly in software systems, which can be used as models for natural systems.

---

[8] Code that describes an object, for example a Dog class, from which more Dog objects can be put on screen. They can be considered as the forms of Greek thought.

c. Logos

We add more details to the listed meanings of *Logos*. The concept became quite elaborate, in theological and philosophical writings; what we pointed are the most used directions of thought, as we will present in 'Greek thinkers' chapter. The narrow dictionary meanings are, per Strong's entry:

> G3056 *logos* log'-os, from G3004 (lego); something said (including the thought); by implication, a topic (subject of discourse), also reasoning (the mental faculty) or motive; by extension, a computation; specially, (with the article in John) the Divine Expression (i.e., Christ). (Hebr-Gr-Eng Bible)

The base 'lego' is mainly 'systematic or set discourse', different from 'rheo' and 'laleo' which are just 'utter', 'speak', per Strong.

In our words, *logos* is like a set of *expressed thoughts*. We note that when two or more persons are expressing their thoughts towards each other, we get a dialogue, term made of from *dia* (Gr. through), and *logos*. In a *system logos*, we may get multi-directional relation between components, like in a dialogue.

According to several Greek writers, *Logos* as *Designer* represents the Spirit through whom all the natural systems came into existence and are maintained. Concerning this, a good compendium is "Development of Logos Doctrine" by Frank Walton (Walton). Theologians throughout centuries discussed much the *Logos* concept. We will address some of these writers. One sample here is from Gordon Clark, professor at Butler University:

> The ordinary meanings of the Greek term, i.e., the list in the lexicon, can fairly well be combined into the idea of thinking, or the *expression of thought*. The English cognate is Logic, the science of valid reasoning. As a Greek philosophic term, *Logos* indicates a supreme intelligence controlling the universe. (Clark, 19)

Lord Jesus shows in John' Gospel an explicit distinction between the term (1) *logos* -as a *grouping of thoughts* with *logical relations*-, (2) the term *remata* -as grammatical word-, and (3) the term *laleo* -as talk-. He says that people will be judged based on His *entire teaching* that He calls His *Logos*. Moreover, *Logos* is presented like an active Judge:

He who rejects Me, and does not receive My *words* (Gr. remata), has that which judges him—the *word* (Gr. logos) that I have *spoken* (Gr. laleo) will judge him in the last day. (John 12:48)

We said that one meaning of *logos* is as a system descriptor containing the *designs* of the components plus their *logical relations*. In above specific case, the *'system'* is an *entire teaching* that contains multiple *thoughts* as components & their *logical relations*.

Layers of logos

Several *system logos*-es can be bound by *logical relations* in a *higher-level system logos*. There are *layers* of systems, each layer building up on the lower layer. Each layer has specific *logical relations*. In Universe, all natural *system logos*-es are bound by *logical relations* in a *Universe Logos*. All natural *system logos*-es have their corresponding *logos*-es in the *thoughts* of the *Universe Designer*.

For example, atoms by *logical relations* build chemical substances, these, using *logical relations* build organic substances, these with *logical relations* build cells, these, with *logical relations* build organs, which with their *logical relations* build bodies.

Also, *social constructs* are systems made of individuals or smaller groups, as components, connected by *logical relations,* making up a *system logos.* Examples are a family, a church, a country, a company. *Systems* can be layered, for example a country has families as components.

This concept of multi-layered *logos*-es in the Greek *thought* is described, for example, by Frank Walton in "Development of Logos Dcctrine" (Walton, 41), mentioned before.

Logos as linguistic description

Our *linguistic description* of *forms (designs) & their relations* is also a *kind of logos*, per Plato[9] and others. According to them, the *linguistic logos* is useful to correlate the outside existence to our mind and also through *linguistic logos* we communicate between us the concepts from our minds.

---

[9] Details and citations in 'Plato' chapter. Here only definitions.

By linguistic descriptions, we relate *forms* outside our mind with equivalent *forms* in our minds and we relate *logical relations* between *forms* outside our mind with the equivalent *logical relations* that we think of in our mind.

The *linguistic logos is essential* for the knowledge of the *logos* for different systems, layers, for the communication between us, to create new man-made systems, and also for the knowledge of the *Logos* as the *Designer* of nature.

The *linguistic logos* is also essential for creating *social systems* (families, companies, churches, countries), where people are system *components* and their dialogues are *logical relations,* together making up the *system logos.* Rules and regulation are the first *logical interactions* necessary to make up a social system. For example, the Mosaic Law established the *social system* of Israel, thus it was their *social logos.*

An example for the logos concept

A kid makes a car from Lego components, based on the *car-logos* (containing *components* and how they *logically relate* to make a car) in his mind.

Then, his father draws a description of the *car-logos* (containing *components* and their *relations*). The description of the *car-logos* is similar in essence with the *car-logos* from kid's mind.

The kid makes also a house, based on the *house-logos* in his mind, with same *components*, but different *logical relations*. The difference comes from the kid's *mind logos-es*, not from the components.

The kid has also a *city-logos* in mind; so, he makes more cars and houses as *components*, and binds them with *logical relations* as roads & bridges to make a city. This is a *higher-level system*.

2. About Part Two: Logos in Science

After learning about the *Logos* concept, we address a few natural and man-made systems to analyze a kind of *logos* in sciences, that is the design of a system through the *expressed thinking* of a Designer, and how each system design analyzed is made of *designs* of components plus their *logical relations*. The statement is self-evident, but we want to underscore that a system is composed not only of components, but also of *logical relations*, these being essential. *Logical relations* are a part of the *logos* concept, together with *designs* (*forms*) of components.

We do this to support the idea that *Logos* is a scientific reality that derives from designers' thoughts in case of man-made systems, and from the Creator's thoughts in case of natural systems. In the chapter "Correlations of Logos and Science", we point to several writers that relate *Logos* with specific sciences. We will relate to *information* science, as *Logos* has an informational aspect. By better understanding *Logos*, we may better understand the statements of John that *Logos* is God and that He entered in the world He created, to bring us grace by His sacrifice and truth by His Word.

We analyze how for a system design there is an *intent* for its use. The intent leads to system and subsystems formation; reversely, the intent helps us to understand a system for which we do not have a design, as a natural system. For this case, the intent points back to an *expressed thinking* of a thinker. He is distinct from the implemented systems but can intervene inside them, as an architect is distinct from the plan of the house but he can enter in the house, or as an engineer is distinct from the engine, but can resolve problems inside.

John writes about the *Logos* as Designer who *expressed His thinking* in all things (systems) made by Him; all systems were made through *logos*, by making *designs (forms)* of components, connected by *logical relations*.

Logos has a *personal* aspect, through the designer, and an *informational aspect*, through the system description. We suggest that the *informational aspect* could be discussed with *information science terms*; we will give some examples.

We suggest that some parts of theology and philosophy referring to *Logos* can relate to software concepts and reversely, concepts from software could be useful for theology and philosophy. In software, we *express our thinking* through *words* to create *designs (forms, or classes[10])* of objects and we use *logical relations* to combine them in systems.

---

[10] *Class* is code that describes an object, for example a Dog class, from which more Dog objects can be put on screen. They can be considered as the *forms* of Greek thought.

B. *Issues addressed*

The *Logos* topic is discussed in theological circles, but not as much at lay-person level. However, the first page of John's Gospel is essential, because in the beginning, or essence (Gr. arche) was *Logos*, thus we all need to better understand the concept. We can have a Christian life without a deep grasp of *Logos*, but it is an essential teaching that is important to know. On the practical side, it can help with our progress in faith and influence.

The understanding of *Logos* helps in debates about creation, oneness of God, Lord Jesus' Deity and incarnation. People come to Lord Jesus because of His love, proved in His sacrifice for our sins. But for discussions about Lord Jesus' Deity, the *Logos* doctrine is important.

In the first centuries, apologists used the *Logos* doctrine for such debates, but when the ideas got clarified, after centuries, the interest at layman level for *Logos* was reduced, as most people in Europe accepted the Creed of Nicaea.

At reformation, the leaders focused on salvation by faith, not by deeds; they did not debate the unity of Lord Jesus with the Father; thus, the *Logos* topic was not important.

In our times, with atheism in schools, connections with polytheists, pantheists, and strict monotheists excluding Jesus' Deity, we need to review how Christians defended their faith in the first centuries. For them, the *Logos* concept was of essence for apology, and we suggest it should be for us at layman level.

We also face the false contrast between science and faith; false because the reality is the same, regardless of views. The *Logos* doctrine was the explanation for both views, and we should get more familiar with it, as we oppose the teachings of the world. In this sense, Paul presents Christ, John's *Logos*, as the source of *wisdom* and knowledge, as opposed to the wisdom of basic principles (Gr. stoikeia, elements).

> 2. (So) that their hearts may be encouraged, being knit together in love, and attaining to all riches of the full assurance of understanding, to the knowledge of the mystery of God, both of the Father and of Christ,
>
> 3. in whom are hidden all the treasures of wisdom (Gr. sophia) and knowledge (Gr. gnoseos).

8. Beware lest anyone cheat you through philosophy (Gr. philo-sophia, love of wisdom) and empty deceit, according to the tradition of men,

according to the basic principles of the world,

and not according to Christ. (Colossians 2:2, 3, 8.)

Next, Paul explains the *wisdom* according to Christ, which is mainly the understanding that:

9. For in Him dwells all the fullness of the Godhead

bodily; (Colossians 2:9)

This is similar with "the *Logos* is God" and "*Logos* became flesh", as John writes. Then:

10. and you are complete in Him, who is the head of all

principality (Gr. arches) and power (Gr. ex-ousias).

(Colossians 2:10)

In the text, we see that by Christ, the *Logos*, we get complete wisdom and explanations to every questions. He is the 'arche' of all 'arches' in the Universe, meaning like "in arche was Logos" from John. He is also the head of all power (Gr. ex-ousias), which puts Him on the same level with God; this reminds us of the Council of Nicaea, which stated in the Creed that the Son is of 'omo-ousias', same substance, with the Father. (Nicene_Creed)

We wish that through this dissertation we would appreciate (as agape) and know better our Lord Jesus Christ, the Incarnate *Logos*, because "This is eternal life, that they may know You, the only true God, and Jesus Christ whom You have sent" (John 17:3), as He prayed.

II. PART ONE: LOGOS BEFORE CHRIST AND EARLY CHRISTIANITY

Apostle John writes his Gospel in Greek, addressing it to people who were aware of the *Logos* concept, thus John does not explain what it means. He will add though values to the meanings. Cultures with other languages were not as much acquainted with the concept. If we want to understand what John is saying, we need to learn what *Logos* meant.

There are many theological studies about the *Logos* background of John's Prologue (the first 18 verses). A couple of examples: Andreas Kostenberger from Baptist Theological Seminary (Kostenberger, 26), Robert Reymond from Knox Theological Seminary (Reymond, 34), George Eldon Ladd from Fuller Theological Seminary (Ladd, 238), Craig Evans from Houston Theological Seminary (Evans, 112).

The possible backgrounds discussed, which do not need to be exclusive, are:

- Old Testament presenting the Word of God and the personified Wisdom
- Greek thinkers
- Jewish thinkers, as Philo of Alexandria, or other writings about Wisdom and an active concept named Memra, related to the Word of God.

As an example, Kostenberger outlines some of these backgrounds:

> (1) Greek philosophy (Stoicism, Philo); (2) the personification of wisdom; and (3) the OT.
>
> (1) In Stoic thought, *logos* was Reason, the impersonal principle governing the universe. A spark of universal Reason was thought to reside within people.
>
> (2) In Prov. 8 (esp. vv. 22-31), wisdom is called "the first of his [God] works," "appointed from eternity, from the beginning, before the world began."
>
> (3) ... the *Word of God in the OT* ... (1) the evangelist ... echoes ... Scriptures ... "in the beginning"; (2) the reappearance of ... terms from Gen. 1 in John 1 ("light," "darkness," "life"); (3) the prologue's OT allusions, be it to Israel's wilderness wanderings (1:14: "pitched his tent") or to the giving of the law (1:17-18); and (4) the evangelist's

adaptation of Isa. 55:9-11 for his basic Christological framework. (Kostenberger, 26)

The above reference to Isaiah is about the work of the *Word of God*:

> So shall My *word* (Heb. dabar, Gr. logos) be that goes forth from My mouth; It shall not return to Me void, but it shall accomplish what I please, and it shall prosper in the thing for which I sent it. (Isaiah. 55:11)

Other theologians emphasize on Greek writings and/or on Philo's vast references to Logos. We will present some of these topics to see precursor concepts related to *Logos*, before Apostle John.

A. Chapter 1 Concepts like Logos in Old Testament

Characteristics of the concept of *Logos*, as presented in introduction, may be noticed in the Hebrew Scriptures, centuries before the Greek writers developed the concept and labeled it with the Greek word *logos*.

1. Creation by Word, per Kinds (Forms)

In Hebrew writings, there is a clear distinction between the Creator and the creation, as opposed to some pantheistic thoughts that mix deities with matter. Also, it is clear that matter was created of nothing, as opposed to theories that there was a basic eternal matter, from which God made complex entities. There are though similarities with the Greek thinking about *Logos*, like that all things are created from the God's thought by His Word and all beings are created per their *kind* – which is like *form* in Greek thinking, part of the *Logos* concept. We address these two similarities.

a. God made all through His Word

In Genesis, we see how the *expressed thinking* of the Creator is implemented in *entities,* He does that through His *Word*, which corresponds to *Logos*. Every stage of creation starts with the expression "God said", for example:

> God *said*, "Let there be light".
>
> Then God *said*, "Let there be a firmament in the midst of the waters, and let it divide the waters from the waters."
>
> Then God *said*, "Let the waters under the heavens be gathered together into one place, and let the dry land appear". (Gen. 1:3, 6, 9)

He continued in the same way with the other entities. Philo, a Hellenistic Jewish scholar (first century), made the connection between Genesis creation by Word and the Greek concept of *Logos,* in many places in his writings; an example: "The Logos of the Cause of all things, by whom the whole world was made." (Philo, Sacr. 8) Also, he writes in *'On the Creation'* how the incorporeal *designs, or forms,* belonging to Elohim' thoughts, called *Divine Logos,* were spoken into corporeal entities:

> The *incorporeal* world then was already completed, having its seat in the *Divine Logos*; and the world, *perceptible* by the external senses, was made on the *model* of It. (Philo, Sec. 36).

Philo wrote extensively about *logos* and the influence of the Bible on the Greek culture. We will address more about him in 'Philo' Chapter.

C.H. Dodd, professor in Cambridge, shows that Lord Jesus Himself connects the *Logos* concept with the *Word of God*:

> *Logos* is used of the *'Word of God'*, His self-revelation to men. In accordance with Jewish tradition, adopted by the Christian Church in general, this is conceived as embodied in the Old Testament. Thus, in John 10:34 Jesus cites from Ps. 82:6 'I said, "You are gods." If He called them gods, to whom the *Word /Logos* of God came...' A similar idea is implied in John 5: 37-8 "You have neither heard His voice at any time, nor seen His form. But you do not have His *Word /Logos* abiding in you..." (Dodd, 266)

Russ Bush, Dean at Southern Baptist Seminary, in his book "Christian Philosophy", comparing viewpoints for the origins of the Universe, states that in Biblical Creation the Word of God was the creating power:

> According to the viewpoint of special creation, the processes of creation were directly related to the power of God's spoken Word." (Bush, 127)

In the chapter for Science, we will present how all natural systems are made of components with *logical relations*, which are like sets of special *words*, that are parts of the *Logos* meaning. Also, we show that as we make from *software-words* some *objects* on screen, in the same way natural systems are made from *special words*.

b. Plants, animals made per their kind / form

The word *kind* (or *type*) corresponds to the word *form* of Plato (Coxon, 3). *Forms*, with their *relations,* make up the *logos* of a system; we address *forms* because they are part of *logos*. The *kind*, or *form*, is the same for multiple similar objects; it is generated from an *idea* of a designer. As a *design* of a house is in the mind of the architect before he makes multiple houses, so the *kinds* of plants and animals were designs in the mind of God. He made creatures according to their *kind*:

> Then God said, 'Let the earth bring forth grass, the herb that yields   seed, and the fruit   tree that yields fruit according to its *kind*, whose seed is in itself, on the earth.'

> God created great sea creatures and every living thing that moves, with which the waters abounded, according to their *kind*, and every winged bird according to its *kind*.

> God said, "Let the earth bring forth the living creature according to its *kind*: cattle and creeping thing and beast of the earth, each according to its *kind*"; and it was so. 25 And God made the beast of the earth according to its *kind*, cattle according to its *kind*, and

everything that creeps on the earth according to its *kind*.
(Gen. 1:11, 20, 24)

Philo says in '*On the Creation*': "The world which existed in *ideas* had ... position in the Divine *Reason* (Gr. Logos) which made them." (Philo, 4)

Idea, as explained in Introduction, is the thought from which a *form* is conceived. We also explained that the *forms* (here *kinds*), with their *relations*, make up a *system logos* and that such *logos* is the *expressed thinking* of a designer; in Genesis, the designer is the Creator.

c. Man made in the image of God

Besides his body which is made in the *kind* of mankind, the man was also made in the *image* of God; the word *image* may be considered like the concept of *form*:

Then God said, "Let Us make man in Our image, according to Our likeness" (Gen. 1:26)

It means that the man was invested with qualities and characteristics from Elohim, as persona, consciousness, decision power, creativity, etc. In this case, Elohim not only 'said' and was done, but also *breathed life* into man:

> And the Lord God formed man of the dust of the ground, and breathed into his nostrils the breath of life; and man became a living being. (Gen. 2:7)

The decision power of man becomes quickly evident, when Adam and Eve decided to go against the logical *Word* of Elohim, who said they will die if they eat from a certain tree.

The origin and the essence of *Consciousness* was and is today the subject of intense research, for example Paul Nunez in *"The Science of Consciousness"*. (Nunez). In Genesis, Moses announces that the source of Consciousness is in Elohim, outside the material world. This thought was also the answer of many Greek thinkers, who presented the concept of *Logos* that transcends from Deity to the soul of humans. For example, about Plato's Sophist, we read an analysis by Martin Heidegger: *"Logos is intrinsic to the Being of man...discernment is carried out in Logos,"*

(Heidegger, Plato's Sophist, 123)

2. Wisdom

Solomon's writings date back to 1000 years BC, before Greeks' thinking about *Logos*. Characteristics of *Logos* will correspond with characteristics of *Wisdom* presented by Solomon. We read that *Wisdom* is primordial, existing before the smallest dust particle (quark?) of the earth, as *Logos* in John 1.1, and takes part in creation, which corresponds with John 1:3 "All have been made through Him (*Logos*)".

> The Lord possessed me at the beginning of His way,
> before His works of old.
> 23 I have been established from *everlasting*,
> From the *beginning*, before there was ever an earth. ...
>
> Or the *primal dust* of the world.
> 27 When He prepared the heavens, I was there,
> When He drew a circle on the face of the deep,
> 28 When He established the clouds above,
> When He strengthened the fountains of the deep, ...
> 30 Then I was beside Him as a master craftsman.
> (Proverbs 8:22-23, 27-30)

We see in this text the concepts explained in Introduction: like the Designer *Logos,* the personified *Wisdom* creates layers of specific *logos*-es through which the created objects come into existence.

Centuries later, some 300 B.C., the Stoic Cleanthes writes similar thoughts about *Logos*:

> You (God) guide the universal *Logos* of Reason which moves through all creation, mingling with the great sun and the small stars. (Stoicism Debate)

We find the topic of *Logos* as *Wisdom* addressed, for example, in *"A Theology of the New Testament"* by George Ladd:

> The concept of personified wisdom also provides Jewish background for the Logos concept. In Proverbs 8:22-31, wisdom is semi-hypostatized. Wisdom was the first of all created things and at the creation of the world, "I was beside him, like a master workman" (Prov. 8:30)
>
> (Ladd, 240)

Also, Andreas Kostenberger in *"John"* considers *Wisdom* of Proverbs as a possible precursor of the *Logos concept*, as mentioned, but we give a larger picture here:

> Another candidate (for John's inspiration) is the personification of wisdom in wisdom literature In Prov.

8 (esp. v. 22-31), wisdom is called "the first of his [God's] works," "appointed from eternity, from the beginning, before the world began." Wisdom was "the craftsman at his side" when he marked out the earth's foundations, "rejoicing always in his presence." (Kostenberger, 26)

Also, *Wisdom* is the *moral, ethical* compass of humans, besides their *logical thinking.* This corresponds to *Logos* in John's Gospel, who is "the true Light which gives light to every man coming into the world." (John 1:9) It refers to spiritual and moral light. *Wisdom* is such light:

> I, *wisdom*, dwell with prudence, and find out
> knowledge *and* discretion.
> The fear of the LORD *is* to hate evil; Pride and arrogance
> and the evil way
> And the perverse mouth I hate. ... I traverse the way of
> righteousness, in the midst of the paths of justice.
> (Proverbs 8:12)

Udo Schnelle, from Martin Luther University, observes in *"Antidiocetic Christology"* that "in Philo, the *Logos* frequently replaces *Wisdom*" and "saves those who are associated with virtue." (Schnelle, 215) . Thus *Logos*, as *Wisdom,* has an ethical aspect, bringing order in the moral world.

In Psalms, we read also how the Lord made all things through *wisdom,* and maintains them:

> O Lord, how manifold are Your works! In *wisdom* You have made them all. The earth is full of Your possessions— this great and wide sea, in which are innumerable teeming things, living things both small and great. ... these all wait for You, that You may give them their food in due season. ... You open Your hand, they are filled with good. ... You send forth Your Spirit, they are created. ... (Psalm 104:24-30)

Such a Psalm is a precursor to the *"Hymn to Theos"* of Cleanthes, a Greek writer from six centuries later, who says, in a similar way, that Theos makes all things through *Logos*. Cleanthes is considered in high regard by *Logos* analysts and we will present him later.

3. *Word of God*

God sends His Word many times to his people in the Old Testament. We address a few places, as examples, where the Word of God appears personified and considered as God Himself.

We do that because John says "the Word / *Logos* became flesh", pointing to Lord Jesus, and in Revelation, John names Him "the Word / *Logos* of God" (Rev. 19:13). The Lord indicates that the Old Testament testifies about Him: "You search the Scriptures, for in them you think you have eternal life; and these are they which testify of Me." (John 5:39) and also "Beginning at Moses and all the Prophets, He expounded to them in all the Scriptures the things concerning Himself." (Luke 24:27)

In general, the apparitions of Deity in the Old Testament are considered by many theologians as the apparitions of "the image of the invisible God" (Col 1:15), i.e. Lord Jesus, who is the *Logos* incarnated; we see these thoughts, for example, in "Dialogue with Tripho" by Justin the Martyr (Justin), "Christ in the Old Testament" by Douglas Van Dorn (Dorn), "Appearances of the Son of God under the Old Testament" by John Oven (Owen). From the last one, we mark the story when Abraham was visited by three angel-looking persons, but One was the Lord, per Owen also "an appearance of God in human shape". (Owen, 16)

Specifically, also the *Word of God* appears to men, and in some cases is considered as God Himself. Douglas Van Dorn points to a couple of instances in "Christ in the Old Testament" (Dorn). We give his Bible citations:

The *Word* of the LORD came to Abram in a *vision*... Abram said, "Lord GOD, (Adonai Yahveh)" ... [5] Then He brought him outside. (Gen. 15:1)

Septuagint (Greek Old Testament, 3rd century B.C.) translates the term *word* with *logos.* It is remarkable how the *Word* came in a *vision*, then there is a change from '*Word* of the LORD' to 'Lord GOD' and how as a being, He brought Abraham outside.

We see Jeremiah having a similar experience:

The *Word* of the LORD came to me. ... 6 Then said I: "Ah, Lord GOD! Behold, I cannot speak, for I am a youth." 7 But the LORD said to me ...Then the LORD put forth His hand and touched my mouth." (Jer. 1:4) (Bible)

Here also, the *Word* is addressed by Jeremiah as God, and then also, He behaves like a human being when "the Lord put forth His *hand* and touched" Jeremiah. It is fascinating how God *expressed His thinking*, then presents Himself as a *being with hands*.

Logos is the *expressed thinking of God*, one with God, in creation and in relation with the man to build the 'new creation'. In the Old Testament, in many occasions the Word of God is revealed to His people; Septuagint translates '*the word*' (Hebr. dabar) with '*logos*' in Greek. God gave His Law as a '*logos*' of society, as the good and correct *logical relations* between people and God, and between men, *spoke* through prophets what are the consequences if people will have *logical or illogical relations* and offers the *Logos* as *Wisdom* to help people to keep His order. God continued to issue His *Word* after creation, with the goal of a new type of creation in the hearts of men, often in a dialogue with the men and taking in consideration their responses. As we explained in Introduction, the *logical relations*, parts of *logos*, are bi-directional, and we see how God has exchanges of thoughts with men, for example with Adam & Eve, Cain, Abraham, and many others. He established the Tent of the Meeting, looking for meetings with men to have a dialogue, and most important, the *Logos* became a man to relate to us, absorbing our failures so we can relate and talk with Him as in a family. With these two-way relations, sure with God having the main part, God choses to give us some choice, so that we can answer Him eventually with respect and love, not just as servants executing orders but as friends.

'God is love' statement binds well with *Logos* that brings mutual *relations*. By *Logos*, love can be manifested, as He came with 'grace and truth'. Thus, we can say 'We love Him because He first loved us.' (1 John 4:19)

B. Chapter 2 Greek thinkers

A major theme for most Greek thinkers, which were philosophers, poets, nature researchers, mathematicians, was the quest for the *essence* of essences, or *arche*, of their specific domains and of the entire cosmos, even concerning the man's soul and the Spirit who created and maintains everything. This *arche* referred to different concepts per different thinkers. As we know, Apostle John declares that 'in the beginning - *arche* was *Logos'*. The quest for a main *arche* indicates a monotheistic trend, in the midst of polytheistic life styles. Adam Drozdek, Duquesne University, USA, starts his book *"Greek Philosophers as Theologians"* noting:

> The interest…in establishing the cosmic *arche*, that is both the *principle* and the *beginning* of the world − … gives rise to a very strong *monotheistic* bias of theological views of most of the Greek philosophers. (Drozdek, Preface)

He analyses, for Greek thinkers before Christ, the concept of *arche* considered as *Logos, Being, Harmonia, Soul, Mind*. During centuries, they learned from each other and in later stages *Logos,* as *expressed thinking of a designer* and *descriptor of forms & their relations,* became the preeminent *arche,* encompassing the others, as we note that *Logos* is generated from *beings* with *soul* and *mind,* and builds *harmonies* by *logical relations.* However, Drozdek ends his book marking that it was not the Greek thinking that continued or solved the *arche* question, but Christianity.

We address here the Greek writers that considered *Logos* as essential, preparing the concept for Apostle John.

1. *Pre-Socratics*

There are several pre-Socratic thinkers (before 4th century B.C.) which use the term *Logos*; Heraclitus (5th Century B.C.) appears to be the first and we address also Parmenides. One example of analysis about these two is *"Greek Philosophers as Theologians"* by Adam Drozdek. (Drozdek, 32, 46)

a. Heraclitus

Heraclitus was a noble from Ephesus (ca. 500 B.C.) who wrote many influential statements, marked as 'fragments". Several refer to Logos, for example:

Fragment 50:

> If you have not listened merely to me, but have listened (in obedience) to the Logos, then Knowledge (which subsist therein) is to say as the *Logos*: one is all.

Above translation is from Heidegger's book *'Heraclitus'* (Heidegger, Heraclitus, 198).

Heidegger, a 20th century philosopher with much interest in Logos, sees in Heraclitus' writings that "this *Logos* is *Being* itself, within which all beings unfold" (Heidegger, Heraclitus, 210) and "the being of beings – *Logos*" (Heidegger, Heraclitus, 241) and *"Being is the Logos"*. (Heidegger, Heraclitus, 282)

Another example of a 'fragment' referring to *Logos:*

Fragment 45:

The extremities of your soul you'll not be able to find, even if you wander down every single path: so far reaching is its *Logon*. (Heidegger, Heraclitus, 214)

Looking at the above two fragments together, Heidegger sees that "the *logos* is the self-announcing all-uniting *One*." (Heidegger, Heraclitus, 216)

In the book *"Fragments of Heraclitus"* by T. Patrick, which analyses views about Heraclitus, we see that

By ancient commentators of Heraclitus, the *Logos* was understood as *Reason*, and in this general sense it is taken by modern commentators. (Patrick, 336).

We mark that it is *expressed* Reason, because the expression *'to say as the Logos'* shows that *Logos* communicates something.

b. *Parmenides*

A poem written by the Greek philosopher Parmenides contains a part referred to as "The way of the Truth" and a part "The way of Opinion". In the first part, he outlines the concepts of *Perception* vs. *Logos:*

> You must debar your thought from this way of search, nor let ordinary experience in its variety force you along this way, allowing the eye, sightless as it is, and the ear, full of sound, and the tongue, to rule; but judge by means of the Reason (Logos), the much-contested proof which is expounded by me. (B 7.1-8.2) (Parmenides)

The writer insists for the judgment by *Logos*, as reason, not by what we perceive about perceptible objects. A system is made of *components & their relations*; recursively, components at their turn, are also made by *smaller components & their relations*. By the five senses, we perceive the physical entities, but by *logos*, as reason, we detect the *relations between components and their design*. After that, the *logos* in our mind reflects the *logos* of the system. We note that *logos* remains when objects disappear.

One example of presentation about pre - Socratic thinkers is at Stanford University: (Presocratic Philosophy)

2. Plato / Socrates

A well-known and very influential thinker, Plato, writes many 'dialogues' with the teachings of Socrates, his professor, who is discussing with peers about his philosophy, which is deemed to be also the philosophy of Plato.

Forms / Idea

The *theory of Forms* is the leading aspect in Plato's thinking. As *logos* represents *forms* (designs) & their *relations*, we need to explain what *form* means. An example of book that outlines this is *"Philosophy of Forms"*, by A.H. Coxon (Coxon 1999).

Plato thinks that perceptible similar *objects* have a common *form* (Gr. *morphe*). For him, *form* means a *design,* or *project* from which *objects* are implemented. Thus, *form* is an *entity* that encompasses characteristics, attributes, functionalities, which define several similar objects. That meaning is different from common English, where 'form' means the external format of an object. Furthermore, similar *qualities* of objects are implemented from the same *quality-form*. For example, a beautiful object implements the 'Beauty' *form*.

Plato uses also the word *idea*, translated often -not very adequately- as *'form'* too; *idea* and *morphe* are often used interchangeably even by Plato (Coxon, 3) although other times the *idea* represents the thinking that leads to *morphe*. The *idea* is the conceptual *intention*, while *morphe* would be as a *design* or *project* from which objects are implemented.

Forms have an *abstract* existence, which is separate from perceptible *objects* that make the *material* world. For Plato, *forms* are *primordial* to *objects*: *forms* came *first* into existence, in an abstract manner, then *objects* were instantiated from *Forms*.

We read in *"Republic"* one of the passages about *forms*:

> There are any beautiful things and many good things...
> We speak also of the Beautiful Itself and the Good Itself
> And so, everything which previously we considered 'many,'
> We now go back and consider each to be 'one' according to [its] *'form'*.
> The former [many] things we speak about as 'seen,' not 'mentally understood'

But *'forms'* we speak of as 'understood', not 'seen'...

We speak of many beautiful things and many good things

And Beauty Itself and Goodness Itself

and so, with all the things which before we considered many

we now consider them again according to a single *'form'* of each, which is one,

and which we in each case call 'that which is.'
(Republic, 507b)

In Plato's Parmenides, 130c, there is a discussion between Socrates and Parmenides about the *form* of men (Plato, 364):

What of a *form* of men apart from us and from all men such as we are, do you think that a *form* of man is something?

In Parmenides 132d, it is stated that the Forms are patterns of the natural objects:

"These *forms* stand as patterns in nature, and the other things resemble them."

Further, they discuss that *forms* would be *entities in themselves*, apart from objects, in Parmenides 135a:

"[We] define each *form* as something in itself."

And they continue, using the term *kind* instead of *form*. Plato, in *"Parmenides"*, equates *'form'* with *'kind'* (Gr. *Genos*), per Coxon (Coxon, 3):

"A *kind* of each thing is something and that each has a *being* in and by itself." (Plato, 129c)

Instead of *'kind'* another translation for 'genos' is 'class' (Plato Parmenides, 1)

The thought that *Forms are themselves real entities* is of paramount importance for Plato, a distinctive thought that sets him apart, and sets apart the philosophies that follow him as 'Idealist', versus 'materialist' philosophies that do not see the existence of *forms*.

We insert now our thought that in Object Oriented Software we write a 'class' that defines a type of objects, then we can make multiple objects of the same class. For example, from a 'horse' class on hard disk describing a horse, we make more horses on screen. So, the 'horse-ness' is an *entity* by itself. This would support Plato's point against those who said that they do not see any 'horse-ness' in a horse. In nature, a class 'horse' can be in the mind of the Designer of horses. We will discuss more about this in the chapter about software.

Forms associate by a Logos of relations

Forms *relate* to each other in *'communities'* (Gr. koinonia) or 'collections', by a sort of *logos*. In Plato Sophist we read:

> Or shall we gather all *things together*, believing that they are capable of combining (Gr. *logois*) with *one another*? (Plato)

In Greek: παρ' ἡμῖν **λόγοις** τιθῶμεν (Plato, Sophist, 251d)

In *"The Classical Theory of Relations"*, Constantine Cavarnos addresses the *relations* according to Plato (Cavarnos, 17). Plato talks of (1) the relation, (2) its opposite, (3) the terms of a relation (meaning the entities bound by that relation), and (4) the ground of relation (meaning the reason inside those entities why that relation exists). Specifically, Plato considers that between *forms* there are relations of *blending, exclusion,* and *otherness.* A *form* blends (or mixes) with another one, or *forms* exclude each other, or *forms* are from other different domains. (Cavarnos, 25)

About *communities,* John Sallis submits in *"Being and Logos"* that there is "a structural relation between *communities* of *kinds* (*forms*) and *Logos*". (Sallis, 507) Sallis expands the analysis in Section 4, *'The Community of Being and Logos'.*

Logos is itself a class (or genos)

Plato observes that *logos* itself is a *class* or *genos* in *"Sophist'*:

Stranger: ... *one thing mingles with another.*

Theaetetus: What was our object?

Stranger: Our object was to establish *Logos* as one of our *classes* of being. For if we were deprived of this, we should be deprived of philosophy; ... we must ... come to an agreement about the nature of *Logos*. (Sophist, 260a)

From the previous two texts, results that the *logos* is the *descriptor* of *objects that combine* (Gr. logois) and of *their combinations* (or *mingling*).

In the above text, *classes* translate the word *genon*. This could be also *genus* in English, which is nearly synonym with *class* or *type* (Coxon, 3).

So, we are told that *logos* is itself a *class*. When more logos-es, viewed as *classes* (*designs* or *forms*), have *logical relation* between them, a higher-level logos is made up. Similarly, a next level can be constructed.

The *logos* of a system is the totality of components' *forms* & their *logical relations, including the utilitarian external logical relations.* Our way of explaining this:

- To *create* a system with novel *utility*, a designer, starting from the needed utilitarian *external logical relations*, designs the *forms (projects) of the components & their logical relations*; all these are called *system logos*. It is generated by the designer's *expressed thinking*, which means his *mind logos*.

- To *understand* a system, man-made or natural, with our minds we detect the *components' forms & their relations*, that is the *system logos*. Then, we can communicate with others about the *forms & their relations*, that is the *system logos*.

This view of Plato represents the lowest level of matter and up to the highest levels of Universe, as well as other associations, like families, corporations, churches, cities, states.

Plato's thinking about God

In the introduction to "Sophist by Plato", Benjamin Jowett notes:

> In all the later dialogues of Plato, the idea of mind or intelligence becomes more and more prominent. That idea … Plato … extends to all things, attributing to Providence a care, infinitesimal as well as infinite, of all creation. The *divine mind* is the leading religious thought of the later works of Plato. The human mind is a sort of reflection of this, having ideas of *Being*, Sameness, and the like. At times they seem to be parted by a great gulf (Parmenides); at other times they have a common nature, and the light of a common intelligence. (Gutenberg Sophist)

Plato maintains that 'Providence', the divine mind, created and maintains the nature, including human mind. He explains how, though we share an ability to create and have intelligence, we are still parted by the extent of our ability to create and the knowledge we have.

In Timaeus, Plato presents how by *Logos* and through *expressed thinking*, Theos generates Time and the Planetary System, by which Time is measured:

> As a consequence of this *reasoning* (Gr. *logon*) and *design* (Gr. *dia-noias* ~ thinking) on the part of God, with a view to the generation of Time, the sun and moon and five other stars, which bear the appellation of "planets," came into existence for the determining and preserving of the numbers of Time. (Timaeus, 38c)

This appears like the account in Genesis, strongly different from Greek mythology. (This Timaeus note is not in thesis)

First opponent of Plato, Aristotle

Disciple of Plato, Aristotle accepts the theory of *forms*, but he thinks *forms* are part of perceptible objects, not separate entities, as a *plan* or *design*, in themselves. Thus, he proposes a material world as primordial. He could not accept that *'forms'* can be anterior and outside objects, as a primordial domain. He could not agree that there could be another realm than the material, another realm in which *forms* could be defined before objects. He says: "The assertion that these *forms* are exemplars, and that the rest of entities participate in them, is to speak vain words." (Aristotle, 36)

To counter him with novel ideas of our time, we can make two comparations: (1) with software development, where *classes*[11] */forms* are previously defined on a hard drive and then *objects* are created when the program starts and (2) with living organisms, where we see how DNA predefines organs and organisms, from which many *objects* of the same *form* are created. By these contemporary science examples, we can extrapolate that natural *systems (objects)* have *forms* and *logical relations* together called *the logos* of systems, which exist before *objects*, in a realm *outside* the world of perceptible *objects*.

---

[11] Code that describes an object, for example a Cat class, from which more Cat objects can be put on screen. They can be considered as the *forms* from Greek thought.

Plato and Aristotle formed schools called the Academy and the Lyceum, respectively. Many people were trained in such schools over centuries and over vast geographical areas, as Alexander Macedon expanded his empire. Alexander himself was a disciple of Aristotle, who was Macedonian too. Their language was not Greek (now in Macedonia is aromana, a proto-Latin dialect), but Greek was the scholars' language.

3. Stoics

a. Zeno

Zeno (4th century BC). founded the school of Stoics. In *"Logos, Philosophy and Theology"*, at Encyclopedia Britanica we read:

> Stoics defined the *logos* as an active rational and spiritual principle that permeated all reality. They called the *logos* providence, nature, God, and the soul of the universe, which is composed of many seminal *logoi* that are contained in the universal *logos*. (Britannica)

In *The Life of Eminent Philosophers,* Diogenes Laertius (3rd century AD) notes that Stoics hold the universe is made of passive matter and "the active principle, *Logos* / reasoning, namely God." (Laertius, 359).

b. *Chrysippus*

Chrysippus, the leader of Stoics after Zeno, says that *logos* pervades all things:

> This is why the goal becomes to live according to nature, that is, according to our own nature and that of the universe, doing nothing that is customarily forbidden by the common law, which is the right *reason / logos* that pervades all things, and is identical with Zeus (Gr. Theos), who governs all beings. (Laertius, 344)

In one phrase, we see a continuous link between nature, universe, customary law, and up to God through the term *Logos*. Some analysts would say that this is close to pantheism, but actually the writer means that *logos* has layers of existence, as John writes too. We read in John's Gospel how in the essence (*arhe*) of all is *Logos,* Logos is God, then al things are made through Him, life is in Him, the light of men - maybe as consciousness - is from Him, He gives the right to become children of God to those who believe in Him, He makes God known, and *Logos* comes into human form. That is not pantheism, is the Unification through *Logos*.

c. Cleanthes

Cleanthes, another Stoic, considers that everything in the cosmos happens according to *Logos*, but evil still happens because of human folly. This thought is found in Drozdek's *"Greek Philosophers as Theologians"*. (Drozdek, 244). (Cleanthes_Stoic)

Cleanthes writes about *Logos* in *"Hymn to Theos"*:

> ...You guide the universal *Logos* of Reason which moves through all creation, mingling with the great sun and the small stars. O God, without you nothing comes to be on earth, neither in the region of the heavenly poles .... For thus you have joined all things, the good with the bad, into one, so that the eternal *Logos* of all came to be One. ... This *Logos*, however, evil mortals flee, ... they neither see nor listen to God's universal Law; and yet, if they obey it intelligently, they would have the good life. Web: (Stoicism Debate) , Book: (Cleanthes_Stoic)

The phrase "the universal *Logos* of Reason which moves through all creation" corresponds with John 1:3 "Through him

/ Logos all things were made; without him / Logos nothing was made that has been made."

Similarly, in "Cleanthes Hymn to Zeus and Early Christian Literature" Johan Thom compares Cleanthes statement "O God, without you nothing comes to be on earth, neither in the region of the heavenly poles, nor in the sea" with the same John 1:3 noted above. (Cleanthes_Hymn, 495)

The phrase "eternal Logos of all came to be One" reminds us of the renown 'Shema' (Hear) which Moses told Israel in Deuteronomy 6.4:

"Hear Israel, YAHVEH our Elohim, YAHVEH is unity (Hebr.: achd)" (Bible)

For Hebrew to English, see (Hebr-Gr-Eng Bible)

We note that for Greek thinkers, Logos is the essence of unity and indicates the one-ness in nature and with the conscious Designer; polytheistic thinking does not perceive such one-ness. In Plato's dialogues, often Socrates insists on the 'One' essence as opposed to 'many' essences. He was condemned to death for teaching people not to worship deities, but to think of the Unifying One. For him, the so-called deities could be from the realm of *created* entities (like angels, good or bad), while *Logos* is beyond created entities and unifies all in an orderly universe.

We observe that the *expressed thinking* and the *logical relations* in nature come from the One who thinks and expresses Himself as a Designer that creates, generates plans for systems (objects), links those plans for upper-level systems, implements systems, maintains them and does much more. For the question "why He does that?" a concise answer is: because 'God is love.' (1 John 4:8)

C. Chapter 3 Jewish thought

1. Philo of Alexandria

Philo was a prominent scholar who wrote many theological works explaining the Jewish culture to the Greeks. He lived at the beginning of the first century, but did not know about Lord Jesus Christ. He was in Alexandria, Egypt, where lived many educated Jews, who studied Jewish and Greek cultures. A book with all his works: (Philo). A link to Philo's writings: (The Works of Philo Judaeus). Abbreviations of his writings, Latin and English: (Philo of Alexandria)

In some of his writings he addressed the concept of *Logos*, through which God created all things and through which all things and dominions are sustained. We comment on a few of the Philo's texts addressed in *"Internet Encyclopedia of Philosophy"* by Marian Hillar (Hillar). All citations are from Philo of Alexandria (Philo).

Philo describes Logos as God

He comments on Genesis about the creation of man, presenting Logos as God:

> It is fitting that the rational soul of man should bear the type of the divine Logos. (QG 2.62).

Logos as the Universal Bond

The *Logos of the living God*, with its aspect of *logical relations,* bonds subsystems (components) to make upper-level systems, in all the Universe:

> For the Logos of the living God being the bond of everything, ... holds all things together, and binds all the parts, and prevents them from being loosened or separated. (Fug. 112).

A similar idea is in the following text; moreover, Philo mentions that Logos is complete:

> And the Logos, which connects together and fastens everything, is peculiarly full itself of itself, having no need whatever of anything beyond. (Her. 188).

Logos as the expressed thinking of God

For Philo, all existence, as atoms, planets, plants, animals, humans with mind and spirit are made through the Logos.

> ... the Logos of the Cause of all things, by whom the whole world was made. (*Sacr.* 8)

> For it is by all means the peculiar attribute of God to foretell what is to happen. And why do we say this? for his Logos does not differ from his actions. (*Somn.* 1.182)

About creation:

> The incorporeal world then was already completed, having its seat in the Divine Logos and the world, perceptible by the external senses, was made on the model of It. (Op. 36)

Philo notes that incorporeal entities are the models (or kinds, or types), like Plato's Forms, of the perceptible corporeal entities, which are like Plato's objects. These incorporeal models or kinds are located in the Divine Logos. God, as a designer, made first the designs of the models in His mind, and then implemented them through His Word / Logos in perceptible objects. Similarly, architects and engineers make a design / model, then make houses and engines from the design / model.

By 'incorporeal' entities, Philo refers to the 'kinds' or 'types' from which God modeled perceptible plants and animals in Genesis 1:

> God said, 'Let the land produce vegetation: seed-bearing plants and trees on the land that bear fruit with seed in it, according to their various *kinds*.'

> God created the great creatures of the sea and every living thing with which the water teems and that moves about in it, according to their *kinds*, and every winged bird according to its *kind*.

> God said: 'Let the earth give life according to its **kind**; cattle, creeping things, and beasts of the earth after their *kind*' (Genesis 1:11, 21, 24).

Philo thus indicates that Moses wrote before Plato about the concept of *kinds*, which is similar with the platonic concept of *forms*. In Stanford Encyclopedia of Philosophy, we read:

> According to a well-attested tradition, some Jews posited that Plato had taken his inspiration from Moses, an idea that seems to have been popularized by Aristobulus of Paneas, a Jewish philosopher who lived in the second century BCE. Philo employs this kind of assertion with prudence, in Spec. 2.164–167. (Stanford_Philo)

For Philo, the Logos is God's Expressed Thinking implemented in created things:

> For God, while he spoke the *Logos*, did at the same moment create; nor did he allow anything to come between the Logos and the deed; one may advance a doctrine which is pretty nearly true: His Logos is His deed. (Sacr. 65)

According to Philo, Logos unites the creative Goodness and the governing Authority of God:

> God ...by his Goodness had created everything; and by his Authority he governed all that he had created; the third thing which was between the two, and had the effect of bringing them together was the *Logos*, for it was owing to the *Logos* that God was both a ruler and good. (Cher. 1.27-28).

Logos as the Wisdom of Proverbs:

Philo considers that the Wisdom of Proverbs 8:22 is represented by 'some one of the beings of the divine company', which phrase is implied as Logos by Marian Hillar *in Internet Encyclopedia of Philosophy* (Hillar). The text of Philo:

> Wisdom is represented by *some one of the beings of the divine company,* as speaking of herself in this manner (in Prov. 8:22): 'God created me as the first of his works, and before the beginning of time did he establish me'. (Ebr. 31),

Craig Evans, in the *"Journal for the Studies of the New Testament"* sums up the characteristics of Logos in Philo's writings:

> The diverse qualities of Philo's logos —advocate, disciplinarian, physician, shepherd, and fountain of wisdom— parallel some of the elements explicitly asserted or implicitly assumed in the Christology of the Fourth Gospel. (Evans, Series 89 pg 109)

We note that the concept of *Oneness of Deity,* with *Logos* as the *Expressed Thinking* and as *system descriptor of forms & their logical relations,* from which all nature and human spirit derives, was prevalent between Jewish learned people in Alexandria. They, as Philo, underscored that Greek culture of Logos has its roots in the much older writing of Moses and Prophets, the Old Testament. It was translated to Greek as 'Septuagint' in Alexandria, at the request of the Macedonian King Ptolemy, 3rd century BC, but had many partial translations before that, which influenced Greek thinking.

2. *Wisdom of Solomon and Targums*

In the Deas Sea scrolls, from 2nd century B.C., there are writings called *"The Wisdom Of Solomon"*, which are not in the Bile canon, different from Proverbs and Ecclesiastes of Solomon. Wisdom appears with characteristics like those of *Logos*, for example:

> For wisdom is a spirit who loves man, and she will not hold a blasphemer guiltless for his lips, because God is witness of his inmost self, and is a true overseer of his heart, and a hearer of his tongue. 7 Because the spirit of the Lord has filled the world, and that which holds all things together knows what is said. (Wisdom of Solomon, i)

Andreas Kostenberger presents some similarities between *Wisdom* and *Logos*, however as he remarks, there are major differences, as John declares that Logos is God and became flesh.

> Wisdom literature built on these notions (Sir. 1:1-10; Wisdom of Solomon). .... . Wisdom, like John's logos, claims preexistence and participation in God's creative activity. Like the logos, wisdom is depicted as a vehicle of God's self-revelation, in creation as well as the law. Yet ..., John's logos differs from personified wisdom in several significant respects. (Kostenberger, 26)

Another Jewish writing, the Targums, a cumulation *oral law* including paraphrases of Old Testament, presents an entity called *Memra* that relates to *Logos* characteristics. A commentator, Daniel Boyarin, explains:

> Memra is an actual divine entity functioning as a mediator. The following examples from the Targumim suggest that the Memra has many of the same roles as the Logos:
>
> Creating: Gen 1.3: "And the Memra of H' (a form of abbreviation for the Divine Name, the Tetragrammaton) said 'Let there be light' and there was light by his Memra." (Boyarin)

He lists then several examples where *Memra* acts as an intermediary between God and men.

It appears that in such Jewish writings there were concepts similar with the Greek concept of Logos; there are suggestions that Apostle John was aware of this culture when he thought of his Prologue, as mentioned in the beginning of first part.

D. Chapter 4 New Testament: Logos as Christ

The *Logos* concept in the Greek culture was developed and understood for several centuries before and after Christ, in Greek and Macedonian provinces and then in the Roman empire.

When Jerome (4th century A.D.) translated the Bible in Latin, called Vulgate, he chose to translate *Logos* as *Verbum*, (*Word*), as in the Latin culture there was no equivalent for the complex concept of *Logos*. He thought of using *sermo,* from which English *sermon* derives, to express a logical set of words. All other languages followed from Latin with 'Word'. We see God's Providence preparing the world for Lord Jesus, the incarnate *Logos*, when the Greek schools expanded in many countries after Alexander Macedon controlled vast regions and the Old Testament was translated in Greek, called Septuagint, in 3rd century B.C. The New Testament was written in Greek, even the epistles to people with other languages, as to Romans, Hebrews and Macedonians (Philippians, Thessalonians). Also, in the New Testament, the citations from The Old Testament use mostly the Septuagint; in it, the Hebrew term *dabar*, meaning *word*, is translated *logos* and it is often used for *'the Word of God'*. Thus, John was acquainted with *logos* also from Septuagint. Timothy Law published in Oxford Academic that:

> Many studies on the New Testament authors' use of the Jewish Scriptures have demonstrated conclusively that the writers most often, if not always, used the Septuagint (Law, 1)

There are also other terms associated with the term *logos*, used in the New Testament, as *form* (Gr. morphe) which is part of *logos, type* (Gr. tupos), *genre or genus* (Gr. genos), which are similar with *form,* (Coxon, 3), *inherit* (Gr. hyp-arhontes), used for a *form* that *inherits*[12] from other *form*. We will look at a couple of them.

The apostles show familiarity with the culture of the time and they address a population which is acquainted with it, by Hellenization in schools, as academia and lyceums, spread in all countries where Alexander Macedon expanded his kingdom, as Asia, Israel, Egypt.

However, we read in the Bible that the apostles went to gentile cities and started the preaching of the Gospel of Jesus Christ in Jewish synagogues, around which there were also 'God

---

[12] As a Cat-*form* inherits from an Animal-*form*

fearing' gentiles, not worshiping pagan deities. Messiah was presented based on Old Testament prophecies, and that was the key for supporting the new Message. The gentiles took the new teachings of apostles and spread it further establishing churches.

1. *Apostle John*

John approached the gentiles by his Gospel using the Hellenistic thoughts about *Logos*, which according to some Jewish writers were influenced by the Old Testament. He used the concept of *Logos* to introduce Lord Jesus in a vertical manner, not historical or prophetical, as the *essence* (Gr. *arche*, translated *beginning*) of the Universe, and as Deity which came as a man to redeem mankind. The known concept of *Logos* was developed even more by Philo of Alexandria, in Lord Jesus' time, without knowing of Him; Philo was a Jew writing in Greek and who understood that culture. He maintained that the Old Testament was God's Word, where the *Logos,* as a special being representing God, was manifested, and through Him everything was created and is sustained. But he did not considered *Logos* as equal with God or able to become a human, as John did. Gerald Borchert, in *"The*

New American Commentary John 1-11" clarifies the main difference between Philo and John:

> The beginning of Gospel needs to be understood in terms not of Philo's view of an impersonal Logos but in terms of the personal and incarnate *Logos* in John. (Borchert, 74)

As such, John gave a new vision about *Logos*, building over what the term meant in Greek thinking, and through derivations from the Old Testament

a. John's Gospel, Chapter 1

Apostle John's divinely inspired teaching from his Prologue, chapter 1, overtook minds and souls as an overarching explanation of everything, from highest Deity to lowest matter. We repeat the meanings of *Logos*, from Introduction (to have them handy):

- *a Designer's expressed thinking* leading to the creation of a new system
- or *logos as* a description of a system (we call it *system logos*), containing the *designs* of its components plus their *logical relations.*

The two meanings are bound, because a specific *logos in the thoughts of a Designer* and the *logos of a system* that corresponds to it are similar in essence. Also, *all logos*-es in the *thoughts of the Universe Designer* and the *system logos*-es corresponding to them are similar in essence. The *Universe Designer's expressed thinking* was considered the *Logos of the Universe.*

The contribution of Apostle John is substantial and decisive. Chapter 1 contains essential statements regarding the *Universe Logos*:

> 1 In the beginning (Gr. arche) was the Word (Gr. Logos), and the Word was with God, and the Word was God.
>
> 2 He was in the beginning with God.
>
> 3 All things were made through Him, and without Him nothing was made that was made.
>
> 4 In Him was life, and the life was the light of men. (John 1:1-4)

A few observations, by verse:

Verse 1. John, through the Divine Spirit, clarifies that he refers to *Logos* as being in the essence or structure (Gr. arche) from ever, because *arche* denotes not only a 'beginning' in time. For some Greek thinkers the *arche* was *Logos*, but for others *arche* was either *mind, harmony, soul,* or other entities (Drozdek).

John clarifies his position. Those considering *Logos as arche* put it as a mediator between an abstract God and matter, while John declares that *Logos* is God and became flesh. An example of commentary about that, from George Eldon Ladd at Fuller Theological Seminary:

> Faced with the usual Greek dualism of God and the world, they (Stoics) employed the concept of *Logos* as a unitary idea to solve the problem of duality. (Ladd, 238)

Distinctively from that approach, John equals the *Logos* with God (Gr. Theos en ho *Logos*).

Robert Reymond, in his book *"John, Beloved Disciple"* clearly states the Deity of *Logos*:

> John identifies the Word as God and, by so doing, attributes to him the nature or essence of deity. (Reymond, 36)

We find out that *Logos* is Lord Jesus, in verse 14 *"Logos became flesh"*. John McArthur notes in his book "the Deity of Christ" that:

> In Him, the true *logos*, who was God, became a man – a concept foreign to Greek thought. (McArthur, 18)

This way, the unity of the Father with the Son is explained through *Logos*, as underscored in verse 2: *Logos* was in essence (Gr. *arche*, translated *beginning*) with God. The term *'with'*, that is *'pros'* in Greek, carries a nuance too. For this issue, we would call attention to information systems (as we use to): we call *proxy* a computer on which a web page is copied from another distant computer, to reduce distances of access (ex. In Europe a system, in America another). The information is the same, but the hardware is different. We can have this in mind when we think about the term *pros* of John.

Ladd, mentioned above, points that John's 'beginning' is before and beyond Genesis' 'beginning':

> "In the beginning" ... This phrase is certainly a deliberate allusion to Genesis 1:1: "In the beginning God created the heavens and the earth." "The beginning" in John 1:1 goes behind Genesis 1:1. At the very beginning of the eternity past existed the *Word*. (Ladd, 238)

Verses 1 and 2 are explanations about *Logos*, beyond eternity. The start from Genesis is equivalent with verse 3:

'All things were made through Him, and without Him nothing was made that was made.' (John 1:3)

Here, John clarifies that the *Logos* is primordial, not the matter, which is made through (Gr. dia) *Logos*. Most Greeks were thinking that some basic matter (water, air, fire, atoms) was from ever and God's *Logos* modeled it by many *logos*-es. John declares, as Moses in Genesis, that all matter was created through *Logos*.

We recall from *Logos* meanings how a system is made from *designs* (*forms*) of components and their *logical relations,* which together make up the *logos* of a system. We know now that even atoms are made of smaller *components*, quarks, plus their *logical relations*. As we cannot divide in smaller pieces forever, some scientists (Nobel Prize 2023) believe that at the bottom there are different energy waves as the lowest *components,* which by their *logical relations,* as some harmonies in a music band, make up localized entities, under quarks. So, *components* with *logical relations* are the key terms to determine a *system's logos*. Even every wave is *logos* based, as it is a manifestation of *logical* oscillations of energy. *Logos* as the *expressed thinking* of the Universe Designer made up all *logos*-es of all systems at any level; nothing was made without

Logos. This statement by negation makes sure there is no escape for the possibility of a primordial matter, and before any matter is *Logos*.

Verse 4. 'In Him was *life* (Gr. zoe)'. The term *zoe* included all meanings of life, as biological (Gr. bios), and mindful life in general.

Biological *life* consists of *Logos*. This was always evident, if someone was looking carefully to the things made by the Lord, as per Romans 1:20. This is more evident today through our knowledge of DNA's logical programming, which is a highly advanced *system descriptor, as a logos.* It has language characteristic, grammar, dictionary, through which the *intents* are clear for different utilities, pointing to an *expressed thinking of the Designer.* George Ladd from Fuller Theological Seminary has a word about this:

> The divine Logos was called ... generative principle of the world. This vital energy both pervades the universe and unfolds itself into innumerable logoi ... that energize the manifold phenomena of nature and life. (Ladd, 238)

Mental and spiritual *life* is directly related to *Logos*, as *expressed thinking* and *communication* correspond to the concept of *Logos*.

Consciousness, that seem to be the *'light of men'* from John 1:4, derives through *life* from *Logos*. Our mental logical abilities, our self-analysis and analysis of the universe, our abilities to judge good from bad, our ability for love through senses and for abstract love, all derive from *Logos*. In our time, as Artificial Intelligence emerged, the quest for understanding Consciousness intensified. A survey of such studies is *The Science of Consciousness* of Paul Nunez. (Nunez 2016). From John's divinely inspired statements, we learn that consciusness derive in living men from the Creator Logos.

With consciousness come abilities to recognise someone; the world did not recognize Him, *Logos*, when He entered the world. With consciousness comes choice; his own did not receive Him, oposing all their prophecies about Messiah. But also through consciesness, led by *Logos*, some people received Him, meaning they 'believed in *His Name'* (John 1:12). When Logos came in the world, His Name was Jah-shua, God Saves, 'for He will save His people from their sins'. (Mathew 1:21) To those who believed in Him as He fulfilled the meaning of His Name, 'He gave the right to become children of God', who are 'born of God'. (John 1:12)

In this manner, we see how the *Logos* plays the most important role on *moral and ethical levels*, not only for the Creation. As He became our representative, He explained us what is good and bad, payed our debt for our bad, taking away 'the sins of the world' (John 1:29) and teaches us & gives us strenght through His Spirit. To do this, He became flesh.

Verse 14:

> And the Word became flesh and dwelt among us, and we beheld His glory, the glory as of the only begotten of the Father, full of grace and truth. (John 1:14)

The *Logos* through whom all were made can become *flesh / human body* and help us to interact gracefully. As an architect enters in the house which was in his mind before, so the Creator Logos can come in His world. These are thoughts from the book *'Biblical Architecture'* (C. Dumitru) of my brother Cristian Dumitru, architect, designer of 70 churches.

The old Greek question of how an abstract logos (with forms & relations) can become a physical entity is overridden here in a stunning way. So stunning that they crucified Him for claiming that He is the Son of God, even after major proofs.

George Ladd, from Fuller Theological Seminary, is quite unequivocal by stating:

> John wishes to emphasize that it was God himself in the Word who entered human history, not as a phantom, but as a real man, of flesh. (Ladd, 241)

As 'the *Logos* became flesh', John the Baptist proclaims that the Lord is before him, and only after this we get the first time in Prologue the Name of Jah-shua Christ - Jahve who Saves, Messiah. He was the One whom Jews expected based on prophecies.

> For the law was given through Moses, but grace and truth came through Jesus Christ. (John 1:17)

The Mosaic Law was a *social logos* imposed by God, written on stones; in the new covenant, the Lord says "I will put My law in their minds, and write it on their hearts." (Jeremiah 31:33) Lord Jesus won our hearts through His *graceful* sacrifice to take away our sins (Gr. amartian – missed-mark), still maintaining the *truth* about what is right and what is wrong. He distributed to us His Spirit and teachings, that is His *Logos*. Ian McFarland, from Cambridge University, in *"The Word made Flesh"* notes that Logos became a man so that God could be loved by men:

God becomes fully and definitively present to the world as one with whom creatures can engage so as to be perceived, and loved by them only as the Word becomes flesh." (McFarland, 74)

The closing verse of the Prologue about *Logos* draws an essential conclusion:

> No one has seen God at any time. The only begotten Son, who is in the bosom of the Father, He has declared Him. (John 1:18)

The first sentence prompted me time ago to check in the Old Testament the so-called apparitions of God. I learned that the One whom "heaven of heavens cannot contain", per Solomon (2 Chron. 2:6), was 'declared' (Gr. exegesato), or presented, through 'the only begotten Son' who is 'the image of the invisible God' (Col.1:15). One example is in Exodus:

> Then Moses went up, also Aaron, Nadab, and Abihu, and seventy of the elders of Israel, and they *saw the God* of Israel. And there was under His feet as it were a paved work of sapphire stone, and it was like the very heavens in its clarity. (Exodus 24:9)

Before this text, the Name of God is rendered as Yahveh several times and after this verse the same. Inside this text only, the Name Elohu is used, singular not plural Elohim, marking thus a distinction.

There are many cases of apparitions and, seeing this statement from John, we can concur with many writers about the Christophanies, like Justin the Martir in 'Dialogues with Tripho, the Jew' (Justin), John Owen in 'Appearances of the Son of God under the Old Testament' (Owen), Douglas Van Dorn in 'Christ in the Old Testament' (Dorn). Jewish teachers before Christianity also considered that a special Being was representing the Deity in apparitions, but they minimized these thoughts after the Christian teachings started, to reduce the possibility that Christ is this special Being.

To sum up, we saw how in the essence (arche) of all is *Logos*, *Logos* is God, all things are made through Him, life is in Him, the light of men - maybe as consciousness - is from Him, He gives the right to become children of God to those who believe in Him, Logos comes into human form and gracefully brings forgiveness and He makes God known. That is an impressive total Unification through *Logos*.

The Prologue about Logos was an essential topic in early discussions about the Deity of Lord Jesus and a major subject leading to the Nicene Creed, accepted by the historic churches and also by the protestant ones. Johann Lange, Bonn University comments:

> The *Logos* doctrine of John is the fruitful germ of all the speculations of the ancient Church on the divinity of Christ, which resulted in the Nicene dogma of the *homoousion* or the co-equality of the Son with the Father.
>
> The preexistent Logos is the central idea of the Prologue. ... *Logos* signifies here ... a person, the same as in ver. 14, namely, Christ before His incarnation, the divine nature of Christ, the eternal Son of God. (Lange, 55)

The important Prologue ends and John continues with the earthly life of Lord Jesus. We stand amazed by our Lord.

b. *Logos as the Word of Jesus*

Lord Jesus Himself affirms that His word / *logos* leads to eternal life, by changing the outcome of judgement for those who believe:

> Most assuredly, I say to you, he who hears My *word* and believes in Him who sent Me has everlasting life, and shall not come into judgment, but has passed from death into life. (John 5:24)

Logos who became a human, as the Designer and Maker of our complex spirits and bodies, also takes care of our forgiveness and eternal life, thus completing His plan.

The Lord shows in John 12 an explicit distinction between the term *logos,* as a grouping of multiple thoughts with *logical relations,* the term *remata,* as grammatical words, and the term *laleo,* as talk:

> He who rejects Me, and does not receive My words (Gr. *remata*), has that which judges him—the *word* (Gr. *logos*) that I have spoken (Gr. *laleo*) will judge him in the last day. (John 12:48)

As mentioned before, one meaning of *logos* is as a *system descriptor* containing the *designs* of the components plus their *logical relations.* In this specific case, the 'system' is an *entire teaching* that contains multiple *thoughts* as components & their *logical relations.*

The Person-*Logos* expresses His thoughts by His teachings-*logos*.

c. *First Epistle of John*

Apostle John addresses Lord Jesus as the '*Logos of life*', whom he met as a Person that he could hear, see, touch:

> That which was from the beginning, which we have heard, which we have seen with our eyes, which we have looked upon, and our hands have handled, concerning the *Word/ Logos* of life. (1 John 1:1)

Here, John reaffirms what he wrote in his Gospel, that in the beginning (Gr: *arche*, as essence) was the *Logos* of life and that *Logos* took a human body. He makes clear that the faith in the Incarnation of *Logos* is from God:

> Every spirit that confesses that Jesus Christ has come in the flesh is of God, and every spirit that does not confess that Jesus Christ has come in the flesh is not of God. (1 John 4:2)

This was and is a litmus test to differentiate teachings. It is also a test for our own faith. This dissertation tries to help with the understanding of Logos becoming human in our Lord Jesus.

d. Book of Revelation

Apostle John writes in the Revelation of Jesus Christ that He is named *'Logos of God'*. It is notable that nobody of that time understood the complete meaning of His Name, *Logos*:

> Now I saw heaven opened, and behold, a white horse. And He who sat on him was called Faithful and True, and in righteousness He judges and makes war. 12 His eyes were like a flame of fire, and on His head were many crowns. He had a name written that no one knew (Gr. oiden — perceived, understand) except Himself. 13 He was clothed with a robe dipped in blood, and His name is called The *Word* of God. (Rev. 19:11-13)

The text announces that He will come again. After the first coming of *Logos* to *'take away the sins'* to clean us, next time the same Person-*Logos* will come to *express his thinking* by a Judgement-*Logos*, to clean His Cosmos.

The Word / Logos of God is essential in Old and New Testaments also for predicting the future. I addressed such topics in my books about Daniel and Isaiah, posted on wordpress.com (T. Dumitru, Daniel) (T. Dumitru, Isaiah).

2. Apostle Paul

Apostle Paul was educated, in Jewish matters and apparently also in Hellenistic culture, by the prominent teacher Gamaliel, and raised in Tarsus, a city well integrated in Hellenic culture.

a. Paul in Athens

Paul spoke at the Athenian cultural arena, Areopagus, as it is written in "Acts of Apostles". In front of the audience, he refers to two texts from Greek philosophical poets:

> For in Him *we live and move and have our being* [a], as also some of your own poets have said, '*For we are also His offspring.*' [b] (Acts 17:28)

The footnotes for above text in the BibleGateway link (Bible), only for NIV translation, are:

a. Acts 17:28 From the Cretan philosopher Epimenides
b. Acts 17:28 From the Cilician Stoic philosopher Aratus

Paul quotes Epimenides (6th century B.C.) from his verses in *"Cretica"*:

> They fashioned a tomb for you, holy and high one,
> Cretans, always liars, evil beasts, idle bellies.
> But you are not dead: you live and abide forever,
> For *in you we live and move and have our being*.
> (Epimenides)

The poet points to the conflict between the materialistic thinking of Cretans, who rejected God, and the faith that *'you (God) live and abide forever'*. As Paul choses to say the last line, he also indirectly calls to attention the atheistic lifestyle of Cretans, thus indirectly questioning the Athenian loose life. He notices that they are worshiping many idols, thus not the One God of heavens, in whom we have life.

Paul connects Epimenides' quote with Aratus' quote (3rd century B.C.), from the verses:

Let us begin with God (Gr. Theos), whom we mortals
never leave unspoken.
For every street, every market-place is full of God.
Even the sea and the harbor are full of this deity.
Everywhere everyone is indebted to God.
For *we are indeed his offspring*. (Aratus)

Paul continues and repeats the idea that we inherit from God, saying:

"Since we are God's offspring…" Here, the term 'offspring' covers the meaning of two words from Greek: *genos* meaning *genus,* like *form,* and *hyp-arhontes* with direct meaning of *sub-structure.* (Hebr-Gr-Eng Bible)

This may correspond with the concept of a *form* inheriting from another *form,* and – as we point in this work- with the software concept of a *class*[13] inheriting another *class* (Ex. a Cat *class* doesn't rewrite the code for an Animal *class,* because the Cat *inherits* the Animal *class*). Seemingly, Paul says that we *inherit* our *genus (class or form)* from God. This directs to Genesis, where God made man in His *image* and *likeness*.

---

[13] Code that describes an object, for example a Cat class, from which more Cat objects can be put on screen. They can be considered as the *forms* from Greek thought.

Because of these meanings, we address these verses because *form*s & *their relations* make up a *logos*.

b. *'Form' concept used for Jesus' nature*

Paul's letter to Philippians outlines an essential teaching about Lord Jesus' nature:

> Let this mind be in you which was also in Christ Jesus, 6 who, being in the *form* (Gr. morphe) of God, did not consider it robbery to be equal with God, 7 but made Himself of no reputation, taking the *form* (Gr. morphe) of a bondservant, and coming in the likeness of men. 8 And being found in appearance as a man, He humbled Himself and became obedient to the point of death, even the death of the cross. (Phil. 2:5-8)

Here, Paul is explaining Deity becoming Human: having God's *morphe (form)*, He became a being with a *morphe* of a servant (not Lord) with the likeness and appearance of man. It is remarkable that in Genesis the man was made after the image and likeness of Elohim. Lord Jesus thus was both in the *form* of

God and in the *form* of man - the two *forms* did not exclude each other.

This may be also a way to explain the unity of the Father and the Son: different beings having the same *morphe* (*form*) of God, with all His characteristics, attributes, capabilities, and everything else encompassed in Deity. In Introduction, we mentioned that *forms*, with their relations, are part of *logos*. This is an additional way of explaining the unity in Deity, besides the explanation through *Logos* in John 1.

About the *Form of God* from this verses, Augustine of Hippo, well-known theologian ~300 AD, writes in *"On the Holy Trinity"* as follows:

> The *form* of a servant was so taken that the *form of God* was not lost, since both in the *form* of a servant and in the *form of God* He Himself is the same only-begotten Son of God the Father, in the *form of God* equal to the Father, in the *form* of a servant the Mediator between God and men, the man Christ Jesus. ...

> In the *form of God* He is the *Word [Logos]*, 'by whom all things are made;' but in the form of a servant He was 'made of a woman, made under the law, to redeem them that were under the law'. (Augustine)

The final point of Augustine is that in the *'form of God*, He is the *Word [Logos]'*, thus relating Paul's text with John's text.

We are glad that the explanations of the Deity of Lord Jesus passed the tests of intense scrutiny, even harsh enmity. Those who understood the *Logos* concept could put the cornerstone in its place, sometimes paying with their life. The early theologians used the *Logos* concept for apologies and against heresies, to explain who Lord Jesus was. On their giant shoulders we stand now, as we fly a plane without knowing aerodynamics. However, it is good to know more about *Logos*, our Lord Jesus Christ, to be able to explain better our faith, as Paul says: 'that I may know Him and the power of His resurrection, and the fellowship of His sufferings.' (Phil. 3:10) Yes, it can come with sufferings, but He is worthy and His eternal love for us is worthy. Glory to Him!

E. Chapter 5 Early Theologians about Logos

After the New Testament times, theologians and apologists developed a vast array of writings on multiple topics, of which most important were:

- The Creation
- The Deity of Christ
- The Trinity

In those discussions, many used the unifying *Logos* to explain the Oneness of Deity, in the midst of polytheist societies, and they explained by *Logos* what Lord Jesus meant saying 'I and My Father are one'. (John 10:30) Such explanations have been addressed in writing and during many councils, of which the most influential was at Nicaea in A.D. 325. After that, there was more stabilization about the concepts of faith, and after Constantine the Great allowed the Christians to worship freely, there were less conflictual debates, as many believed in Lord

Jesus and trusted the decisions of the leaders. A good example of a book addressing such issues is *'The Philosophy of the Church Fathers'*, Vol 1. (Wolfson) But in our times, with so much worldwide communications, as we face atheists, polytheists, rigid monotheists, we need to resharpen our understanding about *Logos*, which was at the beginning of Christianity an important explanation for the Deity of Lord Jesus, for Trinity, and for the process of God's creation.

The concept of *logos* was important also in philosophical discussions, in which the concept was instrumental for:

- The split between idealism and materialism
- The differences between Plato and Aristotle. For Plato, *forms, ideas, logos* were real entities, for Aristotle not. Their followers developed their thinking in accordance with the teaching of these main personalities.

Philosophers were called much later 'idealists' and 'materialists', depending of their belief that *logos* with *ideas, forms & their relations* are real entities in themselves or not.

From first century till our days, many authors addressed the Concept of *Logos*; we note just some of those that we approached:

"Church Fathers" like Justin the Martyr, Clement of Alexandria, Origen, Athanasius, Gregory of Nyssa, Eusebius, Augustine, classical philosophers like Hegel, Kierkegaard, Heidegger, moderns like John Sallis, Constantine Cavarnos, A.H. Coxon, Richard Tarnas, recent theologians like C.H. Dodd, Eldon Ladd, Andreas Kostenberger, Craig Evans, Udo Schnelle, Robert Reymond, Johann Lange, Gordon Clark, Gerald Borchert, John McArthur, R.C. Sproul, Josh McDowell, Werner Gitt, just to name a few (more in Biography and Consulted Sources).

However, we will present only a few Christian writers from the first few centuries, who wrote explanations for theological concepts or apologies for the faith written for non-believers. Their works are, for example, on web at: (Church Fathers), and in an eBook at: (Church_Fathers).

1. *Justin the Martyr*

Justin the Martyr was a theologian and leader of the church, martyred around ~165 AD. Born in Galilee, educated in Greek schools, he became Cristian being impressed by the lives of Christians, in stark contrast to the debauchery of pagans, and ready to go through death for their trust in Lord Jesus Christ. He learned from the Old Testament about the apparitions of Christ and prophecies about Him and explained that extensively in the *'Dialogue with Tripho, a Jew'*.

He was the first apologist, presenting the new Way in two writings to emperors and senate, to defend persecuted Christians, who were not representing a danger as they were taught to love their enemies and thus to put an end to endless revenges. He was condemned to death for accusing the government of lawlessness against Christians. A book with all his works is "Writings of Justin the Martyr" (Justin-the-Martyr).

His Greek studies helped him to show the deficiencies of those teachings, compared with the power of the truth in Old Testament. He wrote about the beneficial influence of the Good News about the *Logos*, Lord Jesus, who is God and became man to pay for men's sin, showing us the love of God. All over his writings, Justin links the concept of *Logos*, used sometimes by Greeks to denote Deity, with manifestations of God in the Old Testament and with Lord Jesus.

For example, the title of chapter 127 makes a plain statement: *'These Passages of Scripture do not Apply to the Father, but to the Word / Logos'*. Then, he lists apparitions of Deity, sometimes as *'the Angel of the Lord'*, and in the following text he links those apparitions to Lord Jesus:

No man, saw the Father ... but [saw] Him who was according to His will His Son, being God, and the Angel because He ministered to His will; whom also it pleased Him to be born man by the Virgin. (Justin, Ch. 127)

Justin makes another connection, between the characteristics of Greek *Logos* concept and the *Wisdom* described in Proverbs of Solomon. The Wisdom is from *'everlasting, from the beginning'* and brings life and light to mankind, like the *Logos* of John. Such description of *Wisdom* is centuries older that the similar concept of Greek *Logos*:

Chapter 56   *Wisdom is Begotten of the Father*

The Word / *Logos* of Wisdom, who is Himself this God begotten of the Father of all things, and Word, and

Wisdom, and Power, and the Glory of the Begetter, will bear evidence to me, when He speaks by Solomon the following: *'The LORD possessed me at the beginning of His way, before His works of old. I have been established from everlasting, from the beginning, before there was ever an earth.'* (Prov. 8:22).   All text: (Justin, Ch. 61)

Through Jews in diaspora, the Jewish writings were translated in Greek, of which Septuagint was a full Old Testament translation from 3rd century B.C., in Alexandria. There are good probabilities that the Greek concept of *Logos* was influenced by Jewish writings.

2. *Clement of Alexandria*

Alexandria, Egypt, was a center where several important scholars developed their writings, as Philo, Clement, his student Origen, Cyril and others. Clement was a theologian born in 150 AD, who wrote a vast array of works contained in *Exhortations*, *Instructor* and *Stromata*. The concept of *Logos* is preeminent in all three. His writings can be found at: Web (Clement_of_Alexandria) used for our citations, or eBook (Clement).

In *Exhortations,* he addresses the polytheistic Heathen, explaining in many ways how there is unity of Deity by *Logos,* through whom all things are made. A sample from *Exhortations* Chapter 1 indicates that the *Logos* took the name Christ, and He is the Creator and the Maintainer of 'our well-being':

> ...We (are) the rational creatures of the Word of God / Logos, on whose account we date from the beginning, for "in the beginning was the Word." ... The Word was from the first, He was and is the divine source of all things; ... He has now assumed the name Christ .... This Word then, the Christ, the cause of both our being at first (for He was in God) and of our well-being, this very Word has now appeared as man ... being both God and man.

In *Instructor,* Clement indicates that the Logos instructs us in His way of life. A text from *Instructor,* Book I Chapter 1, introduces this Instructor as our Lord Jesus Christ, who is the Logos:

> Our Instructor is like His Father God, whose son He is, sinless, blameless ...; God in the form of man, stainless, the minister of His Father's will, the Word / Logos who is God, who is in the Father, who is at the Father's right hand, and with the *form* of God is God. He is to us a spotless image.

Stromata has many topics, in which the *Logos* is the essence through which the discussions reach their conclusions. For example, in an ethical analysis from Chapter 9, Clement points that the our 'rational work' derives from the *Logos* and when one acts against *Logos*, the result is not good:

> If we act not for the Word / Logos, we shall act against reason. But a rational work is accomplished through God. "And nothing," it is said, "was made without Him" -- the Word of God.

3. Origen

Origen was a student of Clement of Alexandria, in 2nd century. His extensive treaties were much appreciated, but for some of his thoughts (as about men's souls before birth) he was considered un-orthodox.

For our study, we mention a paragraph from '*Commentary on the Book of John*'. Origen describes how all things are created through *Logos*, who designed in His mind models, or *forms*, and produced sensible *things* from them:

'In the beginning was the Word / Logos', so … all things came into being according to Wisdom (personified) and according to the models of the system which are present in His thoughts. … As a house or a ship is built and fashioned in accordance with the sketches of the builder or designer, the house or the ship having their beginning (arche) in the sketches and reckonings in his mind, so all things came into being in accordance with the designs … clearly laid down by God in Wisdom. … He left her (Wisdom) to hand over, from the *types* which were in her, to *things* existing and to matter, … (from) their *forms.* (Origen on John, 22)   (Note: 'wisdom' is grammatically feminine in Greek.)

Origen appears to follow the thought of Philo mentioned at the respective chapter, where similarly, the Divine *Logos* designs in His mind models, as *forms,* of the 'incorporeal world', then from them makes the world that we perceive:

The *incorporeal world* then was already completed, having its seat in the Divine Logos and the *world*, perceptible by the external senses, was made on the *model* of It. (Op. 36)

This way of thinking connects to Genesis, where physical animals and plants are made according to their *kinds* (or *forms)* from God's abstract design. A full book with Origen's works: (Origen); on web: (Fathers Origen)

4. *Athanasius*

Athanasius, one of the 'Fathers of the Church', wrote extensively theological treaties in the 3rd century (Athanasius, Complete Works). In an explanation for Creed of the Council of Nicea (325 A.D.), he used the Greek word 'homousios', which means 'same essence' (in text 'the same'), to clarify the relation between the Son / *Logos* and The Father:

> That the Son is not only like to the Father, but that, as his image, he is *the same* as the Father; that he is of the Father; and that the resemblance of the Son to the Father, and his immutability, are different from ours … his generation is different from that of human nature; that the Son is not only like to the Father, but inseparable from the substance of the Father, that he and the Father are one and *the same,* as the Son himself said: The *Logos* is always

in the Father, and, the Father always in the *Logos*.' (Schaff, 1)

In *"On the Incarnation"*, Athanasius extensively develops an explanation of the Deity of Lord Jesus, in terms of the supernatural *Logos* entering in the nature He designed, as an architect enters in the house he designed:

> For this purpose, then, the *incorporeal and incorruptible and immaterial Word / Logos of God* comes to our realm, howbeit he was not far from us before. For no part of Creation is left void of Him: He has filled all things everywhere, remaining present with His own Father. But He comes in condescension to show loving-kindness upon us, and to visit us. (Athanasius, Select Works, Incarnation S8)

He explains at length how *Logos* by His incarnation as man and suffering to death, could take death as the penalty for all men and revive them, giving Himself as a sacrifice for sin and offering eternal life to those who believe; an example:

> For the Word / Logos, perceiving that no otherwise could the corruption of men be undone save by death ... while it

was impossible for the Word to suffer death, being immortal, and Son of the Father; to this end He takes to Himself a body capable of death, that it, by partaking of the Word Who is above all, might be worthy to die in the stead of all, and might, because of the Word which was come to dwell in it, remain incorruptible, and that thenceforth corruption might be stayed from all by the Grace of the Resurrection. Whence, by offering unto death the body He Himself had taken, as an offering and sacrifice free from any stain, straightway He put away death from all His peers by the offering of an equivalent. (Athanasius, Select Works, Incarnation S9)

5. Augustine

Augustine, theologian in 4th century, discusses in *'On the Holy Trinity'* Chapter 7 about Lord Jesus having the *'form'* of God and taking also the *'form'* of servant, as written in Philippians 2:5. (Bible). Augustine writes in Latin, but the Philippians text is in Greek originally, and *form* in Greek is *morphe*, explained in the Introduction.

Christ Jesus ...'Who, being in the *form of God*, thought it not robbery to be equal with God; but emptied Himself, and took upon Him the *form of a servant*, and was made in the likeness of men: and was found in fashion as a man.' The Son of God, then, is equal to God the Father in nature, but less in 'fashion'. For in the *form of a servant* which He took He is less than the Father; but in the *form of God*, in which also He was before He took the form of a servant, He is equal to the Father. In the *form of God*, He is the *Word [Logos].* (Augustine, Section 14).

As presented in the 'Athanasius' chapter, the Creed of Nicea used the Greek word 'homousios', (same essence) for the relation between the Son and the Father. In Philippians, as Augustine comments too, Lord Jesus is 'in the *form* of God', thus the unity is explained by the concept of *form,* for our human capability of understanding. It is interesting how He takes also the *'form* of a servant', but kept the *'form* of God' even if He limited Himself.

6. Eusebius

Eusebius was a renown historian and theologian in Eastern Roman Empire, named Romania, per (Byzantine_Empire), in the time of Constantine the Great who supported Christianity (4th century). He wrote an extensive *"Church History"* (Eusebius, History of Christianity). In it, he included valuable apologetic remarks. In his book, there are references to Christ the *Logos*, for example:

> For who beside the Father could clearly understand the Light which was before the world, the intellectual and essential Wisdom which existed before the ages, the living **Logos** /Word which was in the beginning with the Father and which was God ...which was before every creature and creation visible and invisible,... the creator, with the Father, of all things... the true and only-begotten Son of God, the Lord and God and King of all created things... as it is said ... of his divinity: 'In the beginning was the Logos /Word, and the Logos was with God, and the Logos was God.' 'All things were made by him; and without him was not anything made.' Web: (Eusebius, Church History, Ch. 2.3)

Above, he relates *Wisdom* to the *Logos* presented in John 1, and further he explicitly equates the two, indicating that the characteristics of *Logos* are similar with the characteristics of *Wisdom* from the Proverbs of Solomon (Prov. 8). He samples a part of the chapter, but the entire description of *Wisdom* in Proverbs corresponds with the Concept of *Logos* developed by ancient Greek thinkers and with the presentation of *Logos* by the Apostoles, as we analyzed before.

...which is called the Word of God and Wisdom, we may learn ... from the mouth of Wisdom herself: (citing Prov. 8:15) "I, Wisdom, have dwelt 84 with prudence and knowledge, and I have invoked understanding. Through me kings reign, and princes ordain righteousness. Through me the great are magnified, and through me sovereigns rule the earth". (Eusebius, Church History, Ch. 2.14)

Eusebius implies that also in Genesis, the *Logos / Word* partakes at the Creation. He says that Moses, the most ancient prophet, led by God's Spirit presents to mankind how Elohim / God created the world through His *Word*:

Moses declares that the maker of the world and the creator of all things yielded to Christ himself... his own clearly divine and first-born *Logos* /Word, the making of inferior things, and communed with him respecting the creation of man. For, says he, 'God said, let us make man in our image and in our likeness.' (Eusebius, Church History, Ch. 2.4)

Eusebius gives several instances where Lord Jesus appears in Old Testament as a *messenger* (communicator) of God, in the chapter II, named *'Pre-existence and Divinity of Our Savior and Lord Jesus Christ'*.

A major observation is that Eusebius considered, along with other early Christian apologists, that the Greek philosophers "had obtained their wisdom from the ancient Hebrews." (Eusebius, Church History, Ch. 2 Note 48)

III. PART TWO: CORRELATIONS OF LOGOS WITH SCIENCE

In previous chapters we analyzed the concept of *Logos* from multiple historical perspectives, and now we address it from a science perspective, to see how these two views correlate.

We saw how the Logos concept was developed in Greek culture, but also how a similar concept can be found in the Old Testament, much emphasized by Philo. Then, Apostle John completed the explanation by declaring that Logos is Theos, and He became man to redeem mankind. Early theologians explained the Deity of Lord Jesus on the account of *Logos*, and we need in these days to be well aware of such explanations, as we face major debates, including with the scientific materialistic worldviews.

As we gathered till now in our study, in a quick review, the *Logos* is *a designer's expressed thinking* leading to the creation of a new system, made up of *designs of its components* plus their *logical relations,* and *Logos* is also the *description* of such a system. We called the description *'system logos.'* We marked that a specific *system logos* and the corresponding *logos in the thoughts of a designer* are similar in essence.

A human designer expresses ideas on a visible project, or design, out of which a *system* is made from *related components*. We can say that the design is the *system logos*; we keep stressing that *relations* are essential.

For example, architects, engineers make projects of systems; if anybody else wants to understand a system, he looks on the project, or if he does not have it, he can reverse-engineer the system to see its *components and their relations*.

A natural system does not have a visible project (design). We reverse-engineer such a system to see its *components and their relations;* all these taken together make up a *natural system logos*.

As an example, Anatomy (Gr. 'cutting up') explains how to dissect a body to see its organs; in the process of cutting, we eliminate the *logical relations*, but they are *essential* for the body.

A heart and a lung work together by *logical relations* to make up the *respiratory system*. Its *description* can be called *Respiratory System Logos*.

In our minds, we detect that natural systems have *logos*-es, and also by inference from man-made systems we can say that natural systems have *logos*-es. Then, we can state that a *logos* of a specific *natural system* has a corresponding *logos* in the *thoughts of the Universe Designer,* and they are similar in *essence*.

All natural *logos*-es with their *logical interactions* make up the *Universe System Logos*. This has a corresponding *Universe Logos in the thoughts of the Universe Designer.*

From this panoptic, we can say that all these concepts have much to do with Science. There are many writings about the relations between Science and Theology, from early Christianity to our times; we look specifically about *Logos* and Science.

The Greek *Logos* culture, including areas relative to sciences, was further developed for centuries after Christ in the Eastern Roman Empire, where Greek was the language of the schools. An example of a remarkable writer is Maximus the Confessor, from 6th century, who addressed the Main *Logos* and the *logos*-es in created things; an extract:

The natural law ... is directed by *logos* ... through the physical phenomena ... which are interconnected ... in the Universe. It (natural law) has *logos*-es ... and from these, the *Logos* ... is rendered legible when He is read by us. (Confessor, 195)

We will discuss aspects of *contemporary* science (as stated in the title) about *logos* as the essence of matter and about man-made *systems logos*-es.

The larger context of our discussion is the general debate between science and religion, addressed in many studies; one example is "The Reason for God" by Timothy Keller (Keller).

A special case is the *information systems* science; the concepts used in information systems can be useful for modelling *natural systems,* themselves based on *information*. We mention that there are scholars who address specific sciences in correlation with the concept of *logos*; some examples of such studies are about: physics (MESKOS), phycology (Kuhlewind), linguistics (Schrock), education (Yegge).

Before looking into specific systems where *logos* is essential, we review with reverence an important declaration of Apostle Paul about our Lord Jesus Christ, the *Logos*. We read how all things are created through Him, natural and social systems, the Church included, which is the new creation - the actual goal for which the nature was created. In the new creation, through Logos, God expresses His love (Gr. agape) and hopes for love back; Lord Jesus was asking Peter 'do you love Me?' To inspire this love-based relation, beyond a logical relation, God gave His Son to remove our judicial condemnation and thus to win our hearts:

> Giving thanks to the Father who has qualified us to be partakers of the inheritance of the saints in the light. He has delivered us from the power of darkness and conveyed us into the kingdom of the Son of His love, in whom we have redemption through His blood, the forgiveness of sins. He is the image of the invisible God, the firstborn over all creation. For by Him all things were created that are in heaven and that are on earth, visible and invisible, whether thrones or dominions or principalities or powers. All things were created through Him and for Him. And He is before all things, and in Him all things consist. And He is the head of the body, the church, who is the beginning, the firstborn from the dead, that in all things He may have the preeminence. (Col. 1:12-18)

Every phrase is a key statement. Beyond the scientific meaning of *Logos*, there is the *Logos* who came to give Himself out of love for us. Everyone who studies science should build his house on *Logos, the cornerstone.* If someone rejects *Logos,* his house won't stand the tests. So, we will build our next portion of the study on the cornerstone, the *Logos.*

A. *Chapter 1 Logos as the Essence of Matter*

In our times, the attention of many scientists is set more and more on the *informational* aspect of the matter – in its inorganic, organic or biological states. The *information* concept correlates with the aspect of *Logos* as the *expressed thinking* of a designer and as a descriptor of a system, made of components and their *logical relations*.

A new interesting trend was set by Luciano Floridi, from Oxford University, who developed the theory of *'Informational Realism'*, on top of what was known as *'Structural Realism'* (where real entities are some sort of structures). In his analysis, real entities are fundamentally *information* based. He says:

> Informational Realism is ...a solution to a problem. The problem is deceptively elementary: what is the ultimate nature of reality? The answer is misleadingly simple: it is informational. (Floridi)

A great lecture about the *informational* aspect of the matter is *"In the beginning was information"* by Dr. Werner Gitt, head of Department of Information Technology, Braunschweig, Germany. He determines that there are five layers of information - statistics, syntax, semantics, pragmatics, purpose - and shows how they are found in material systems, but cannot be of material origin.

In *biological systems*, he notes multiple aspects of the DNA code that make it an informational system. It has four letters, 'words' have three letters, there is a 'dictionary' of 'words' pointing to amino-acids, from which proteins are built based on DNA's words order, and it "uses structural units like expressors, repressors, and operators." (Gitt, 97)

In *organic matter,* the *information* is obvious in the DNA language. At Creation.com we read:

> "Like spoken languages, biological language is irreducibly and yet without physical substance. It comes complete with symbols, meanings for those symbols, and a grammatical structure for their interpretation.... Physics has nothing to do with symbols or grammar, and therefore nothing to do with the origin of life, which cannot exist without its coded information." (Thomas)

Inorganic matter appears to be based on *information* in many research studies. We note a couple:

A compendium with several studies is: *"Information and the Nature of Reality"* by Paul Davies. As an example, we select the statement: "Physicists suggest theories of reality in which *information* takes over the role that matter once played" (Davies, 73) from Wheeler and Zeilinger studies.

In *"Reality Is Not What It Seems"* a renown quantum physicist, Carlo Rovelli, proposes a *relational* interpretation of the theory of quantum mechanics:

> In … quantum mechanics there is no reality except in the *relations* between physical systems. It isn't *things* that enter into *relations* but, rather, *relations* that ground the notion of *"thing"*. … Quantum mechanics is *not a world of objects: it is a world of events.* … A stone is a vibration of quanta that maintains its structure for a while, just as a marine wave maintains its identity for a while before melting again into the sea. (Rovelli, 135)

He states like Luciano Floridi above:

> Many scientists today suspect that the concept of *'information'* may turn out to be a key for new advances in physics. (Rovelli, 239)

Here are some examples of considering the concept of *Logos* in the natural world. We keep in mind that 'all things were made through Him (Logos)' (John 1.3). Our clear intent is to show that particular *logos*-es can only be the result of an *expressed thinking* of our Designer.

Applicable entities are at all layers of existence. Any system is made of subsystems with their *logical relations*, down to the energy waves making up particles, the inorganic and organic matter, living organisms, and the entire universe.

Sub quarks world:

We cannot divide ad infinitum pieces in smaller pieces. Many physicists think of a kind of 'waves' at low-low levels, which get grouped together through *logical relations,* in essence a kind of *information*, to implement particles, up to quarks. The Nobel Prize in 2023 for Physics was for such research:

> A theoretical framework that describes how different states of *matter may be described by fluctuating fields, analogous to magnetic and electric fields.* (Nobel Prize 2023)

In mathematics, the *'Fourier transform'* theorem shows how every function can be composed from a set of correlated sinusoids. Similarly, at the bottom of matter, a 'particle' can be a set of waves with *logical relations* between them. We suggest that waves, like sinusoids, are repetitive functions; so, if a particle is created by a set of waves, in its description we need only the parameters for the *relations* between waves and their frequency, but NOT 'time'. At the bottom level of the matter the time could be meaningless. Just our thought.

The *system logos* of a particle is made up of *waves* as *components* and of their *logical relations*. It can only come from the *expressed thinking* of the Designer, from His *Logos*.

In sub-particles physics there are no more *material* entities, but *energy* waves. Even every single wave is *logos* based, because it is a *logical oscillation* of energy. We know it is logical, not random, because of the impressive stability of the particles.

Quarks:

Quarks are particles which with their *logical relations* make up protons and neutrons inside the *nuclei* of atoms. Quarks in my body are similar with quarks on the moon, so they have the same *form,* which resides and was developed in the mind of the Designer. The same *form* got implemented in all universe, but not by copying each other. How that multiplication happened, we do not know.

The system *logos* of a nucleus is made up of quarks as *components* and of their *logical relations*.

Atoms:

Different *logical relations*, described through math and physics, connect a nucleus and electrons to make up atoms. Atoms have a certain number of *forms*, per Mendeleev table, and the same *forms* are found in San Diego and Atlanta. They did not copy each other. There must be a *common form* in some place, as in the mind of the Designer.

The system *logos* of an atom is made up of a nucleus and electrons as *components*, and of their *logical relations*.

Molecules, inorganic, organic:

Atoms with *logical relations* make up molecules. The organic molecules are the building blocks of living organism. Organic molecules play a precise role; their *internal logical relations* define the role. Individual atoms that make up these molecules do not have in themselves *information* about the intended role. The information about the *logical relations* needed for the role is outside, *abstract, not embedded in atoms, the order is abstract*.

The system *logos* of molecules is made up of atoms as *components* and of *their logical relations*.

DNA:

The DNA genetic code is made up of four types of molecules that are threaded one after the other. Their order dictates how proteins, cells, and the body are made. (Encyclopedia Britanica) The order is not to be found inside molecules, but it is *external, abstract.*

The system *logos* of the DNA genetic code is made up of four types of molecules as *components* and of *their logical relations*.

Proteins:

Proteins are systems made of amino-acids (biochemical substances) ordered based on RNA (part of DNA).

The system *logos* of the proteins is made up of amino-acids as *components* and of *their logical relations*, extracted from RNA.

Cells:

Proteins and other parts, through *logical relations,* make up *cells*; proteins combine by *logical relations* for a specific *intent.*

The system *logos* of cells is made up of proteins and other parts as *components* and of *their logical relations*.

Organs:

Cells through their *logical relations* make up organs with specific use. Each organ has an inner structure with a clear intention, but also interfaces with other organs.

The system *logos* of organs is made up of cells as *components* and of *their logical relations*.

Bodies:

Organs through their *logical relations* make up bodies. Organs cannot exist independently; the phrase 'irreducible complexity' refers to the impossibility of an organ evolving on its own, without the other organs with which it *interacts logically* to implement a body. (Irreducible Complexity)

The system *logos* of a body is made up of organs and other entities, as *components* and of *their logical relations*.

Brains:

Neurons and synapses link through *physical logical relations* to make up a physical brain. *External logical relations*, with other humans, the environment, etc. are also influencing the structure of the brain. Memories, sensorial input, speech, algorithms of behavior, beliefs based on external or internal thoughts, are some influencers of the brain.

The system *logos* of a physical brain is made up of neurons as *components* and of *their physical logical relations, the synapses.*

Plants and animals' associations:

In a forest, plants as *components* plus their *relations* make up an eco-*logical forest logos*. Animals communicate in many ways, living together in groups that help each other, counter the narrative of 'survival of the fittest'. They have a *group logos,* made up of individuals as *components plus their relations*. In some cases, as ants or bees, the *group logos* is very complex; they have *distributed logos* and behave together as having one group brain.

Universe:

Planets and a star, through their *logical relations* make up a planetary *system*. More planetary systems through *logical relations* make up galaxies, and so on.

The system *logos* of a planetary *systems* is made up of planets & a star as *components* and of *their logical relation.*

We insist to clarify that *logical relations* are essential for system design; we do not *see* them, they come from the mind of the designer and they are captured and explained in the project of the *design*. If somebody reverse-engineers a system, by disconnecting parts to learn from what it is made, he can use some senses to perceive the components, but not the *logical relations*, making up the *system logos*; these are only perceived by *thought* (or from the project, for man-made systems).

In the letter to Hebrews, we are told that faith (Gr. pistis – conviction) is a conviction about what cannot be *seen*, but can be *thought* of.

> Now faith is the substance of things hoped for, the *evidence* of things not *seen*. ... By faith we *understand* that the worlds were framed by the Word of God, so that the things which are *seen* were *not made of things which are visible*. (Hebrew 11:1)

A natural system is made up of *visible* components plus their *invisible logical relations*. Components are also (sub) systems, made up of lower-level components plus their *invisible logical relations*, down to the bottom level of *invisible energy waves*.

Also, the *design* (*form*) of a natural system is not visible, but we can think of its goals, proprieties, qualities.

In a man-made system, as we will present, the *design* is accessible in projects.

B. Chapter 2 Logos in Man-made Systems

Humans, by *expressed thinking*, create a *system logos* from components designs, as *forms,* plus their *logical relations, as* needed for the *goal*. We present a couple of domains:

Architecture:

An architect, by *expressed thoughts,* designs a *house logos* from bricks as *components by their forms* plus their *logical relations.* The builders can make multiple houses (as systems). He designs as needed for the *goal* in his mind. He can enter in a house he made.

Engineering:

An engineer designs an *engine logos* from pistons, cylinders, spark-plugs as *components* with specific *forms* plus their *logical relations.* The *engine logos* in his mind was directed towards the *goal* of making a moving system.

Telecommunication engineering:

A telecommunication engineer designs a *communication system logos* from radio-stations and cell-phones as components plus their *logical relations*. Each sub-system cannot work by itself, but the technical messages between them make them behave together as a system, useful for human messages.

Software engineering:

In software, engineers *express their thinking* by designing a system (for example, a game) from *components* (as cars, houses) plus *their logical relations,* together making up the *game system logos*.

The difference here is that *logical relations* are not only described on paper, as in previous examples, but their description can be *captured* in the program itself. That is, programmers write code also for *relations*, while architects describe *relations* on paper only, they are not physical entities in physical houses.

Hardware, electronics engineering:

The *Hardware* is also designed through software, with Hardware Development Languages (HDL). There are software libraries with *classes*[14] for components (transistors, resistors); the designer connects them through *logical relations,* which are code functions, to make up an electronic circuit / system. The code is sent to the factory to build the integrated circuits.

The components' *classes,* as *forms,* plus their *logical relations* make up the circuit / system *logos*.

Artificial Intelligence:

Artificial Intelligence refers to multiple domains, like *pattern recognition, neural networks, logical languages*. About *pattern recognition*: memorized patterns are compared with a newly detected pattern to see if it matches. It can be used for images, behavioral patterns, words & phrases, gaming patterns, meteorology patterns, etc. Also, reversely, saved patterns can be used to express or communicate; for example, a computer can paint a flower or generate spoken words. The memorized patterns can be considered as *forms* in platonic terms, supporting that philosophy; thus, we can extend the pattern concept from man-made systems to natural systems.

---

[14] Code describing a component

Games:

Games can also be seen as systems made of *components* plus *logical relations.*

Chess is made of pieces plus the rules of movements and strategies, also specific strategies for each play. We see the pieces, but we perceive only mentally the invisible rules and strategies, that can be written on paper.

LEGO constructions are made of pieces plus *logical relations* for a specific project. A kid can make a house or a car from the same pieces plus different *logical relations*, as *expressed by his thinking.*

A *theater* is a system made with people & needed objects, as components, plus *logical relations*, from the play script, together making up the *theater logos*, as derived from the *expressed thinking* of the author.

Tennis is a system made of players, rackets & net & ball, as *components, plus logical relations* as rules and strategies; together, they make up the *logos* of the tennis game.

With these games we train our minds to learn *patterns of thinking*, in the sense of *forms* with *logical relations* -that is types of *logos*- which could be applied in real life.

Families, churches, companies, states:

More people, as *components*, with their *logical relations* based on speech make up an *association logos*, with a specific *intent*. We have grammars, laws, ethics, *to keep the logical relations* in a good state and we have error correction methods to repair broken *(illogical) relations.*

Examples

Family example*:* A man, a woman, then children, plus their *relations* make up a family system, with a family *logos*.

About the first wedding, of Adam and Eve, we read:

> A man shall … be joined to his wife, and they shall become one flesh. (Genesis 2:24)

About the last wedding in the Bible, of the Lord and His Church, we read:

> Then I, John, saw the holy city, New Jerusalem, coming down out of heaven from God, prepared as a bride adorned for her husband. (Revelation 21:2)

The Bible starts with a family *logos* and ends with another family *logos*. What is in between? The Lord built *relationships* around the tabernacle of meeting, but we, men, did broke them; then, *Logos* became man to remove our condemnation by His sacrifice and won our hearts, to bring us in His family. We can now say 'we love You Lord, because You loved us first!'. I wrote a paper on this topic for my son's wedding, posted at (T. Dumitru, Edge Observations).

Church example: several persons coming together with *relations* as presented by Apostles make up the 'body of Christ', which we call here *church system*:

> Speaking the truth in love, (you) may grow up in all things into Him who is the head—Christ— from whom the whole body, *joined and knit together* by what every joint supplies, according to the effective working by which every *part* does its share, causes growth of the body for the edifying of itself in love. (Ephesians 4:15)

We see that the body is '*joined and knit together*', as by *logical relations* between *parts*, or *components*, which is the meaning of *church system logos*.

State example: the Hebrews, *as components,* with their *logical relations* of the Mosaic Law, make up the Israel nation as a *system logos*. Nations that get organized by 'the rule of law', where no person is above the law, follow the Mosaic pattern.

As a *conclusion* from the above list: we state again that the *description* of every *system,* meaning its *logos,* contains the *forms of components and their logical relations*. In the case of a *man-made system logos*, it originates by *expressed thinking* from the corresponding *logos* in the mind of a designer.

Similarly, when we observe a *natural system logos* and make a model of it in our mind, we understand clearly that it also originates by *expressed thinking* from the corresponding *logos* in the mind of our Great Designer. All natural system *logos-es* connected by *logical relations* make up the *total natural system Logos,* implemented as the Universe. This total *Logos* originates by *expressed thinking* from the *Supreme Logos* in the mind of our Great Designer. *Supreme Logos* is one with the Great Designer, as John teaches us in his Gospel. The above ideas relate well with Paul's writing to Romans:

> What may be known of God is manifest in them, for God has shown it to them. For since the creation of the world His *invisible* attributes are clearly *seen*, being understood by the things that *are made*, even *His eternal power and Godhead*. (Romans 1:19)

The Word of God is clearly saying that we can *see* His *invisible* attributes, with our capacity to see with our mind. By looking to the systems which He made, we detect their *logos, with logical interactions* not visible with the eyes but visible with the mind.

We note that we have descriptions of different types of *logos* in specific domains, as 'logy', such as zoology, biology, metrology, astrology, philology, sociology, theology, apology. Most people in Hellenized countries learned about the specific *logos* of different domains and also about the *Supreme Logos*. Apostle John addressed them in their terms, and added that *Logos* is God and He became human, to get humans back on track by taking their load of condemnation. John adds also that the Lord is sending His Spirit to remind them and us about His *expressed thinking,* as His spoken *Logos*:

> The Helper, the Holy Spirit, whom the Father will send in My name, He will teach you all things, and bring to your remembrance all things that I said to you. (John 14:26)

Thus, between us and the Lord there are also *logical relations,* we form a communication *system Logos*. In the Old Covenant, the *relations between God and men* took place mostly in the tent of the *meeting;* in the New Covenant, nobody comes to the Father except by Lord Jesus, the *Logos*, and He gave us the Holy Spirit through whom *we relate with the Father*.

C. Chapter 3
Correlations with
Information Science

Besides the man-made systems discussed before, Information Science plays a special role in our analysis.

The *logos* concept is for a good part an *informational* concept; we propose that software *informational concepts* could be helpful for discussing about it.

The informational aspects of *logos* derive from its most important meanings, which we bring again to attention:

- *a Designer's expressed thinking* leading to the creation of a new system
- or *logos* as a *system descriptor* (*system logos*), that contains the *designs* of its components plus their *logical relations*.

Expressed thinking is informational because it delivers information to create a system.

A *system logos* is informational because it contains information for the *designs* of its components and for their *logical relations*.

The *information* in the *expressed thinking* is similar with the *information* in the *system logos.*

It is important to underscore that the *origin* of information is a Designer as a person, with consciousness, will, desires, intent, memory, etc., who uses certain languages; this applies to man-made or natural systems. Gitt addresses this in *"In the beginning was information."* (Gitt)

As a general note, at Stanford Encyclopedia of Philosophy there is a short overview about using computational concepts for this domain. We cite from the introduction:

Computational philosophy is ... a set of computational techniques applicable across many philosophical areas. (Patrick Grim).

In software, the development process called Object Oriented Modeling (Jacobson) uses *classes*[15] (code describing an entity) & *their relations. Classes* can be considered as the *forms* of Greek

---

[15] Code that describes an object, for example a Dog class, from which more Dog objects can be put on screen.

thought. We will show how this model could be useful for discussions in the *Logos* domain.

When I studied Greek thinkers and theologians debating about the *Logos* concepts, I noticed that some polemics could have been easier clarified by using terms from *information* systems, because, as noted, *Logos* has an *informational aspect,* as descriptor of components' *classes* and their *relations.*

1. *Object-Oriented Design and Logos*

In software development, there is much discussion about the similarities between *forms* in Greek thinking and the concept of *class* as used in Object-Oriented Design (OOD) - a modality of development. Some discussions: Richard Farrar (Farrar), Sean Para (Para 2018), Nick Vennaro (Vennaro). We recall that *forms* (as classes) & *their relations* make up a *logos,* the subject of our study.

We will present some OOD terms, in layman talk, then we will explain theological concepts using OOD terms.

A *class* code has attributes & functions of an entity (ex. a *dog class* has an attribute *color*). A *class* is code on hard-disk; it is used to instantiate multiple *objects* on screen (ex. *dogs* with different *colors*). C*lasses* correspond to *forms*.

One *class* can *inherit* an upper class, like a *form inherits* an upper *form.* For example, a class code 'Tiger' inherits the class code 'Feline', does not repeat it. A class can inherit *multiple* upper classes, like a 'Tiger' class inherits a 'Feline' class and a 'Circus Animal' class.

More objects of the same class are *equal* by attributes & functions, even if the *values* of attributes are different. For example, two dogs are equal by attributes & functions, even if the color differ. There are specialized *equality-operators* for different entities.

Communication functions, or logical relations, between *classes* are used between objects on the screen (like when *dogs* on screen play together). We call them *'dialog'* [16].

The *Coordination* of dialogs is an operation needed when multiple entities relate. This keeps the *communication* in the right order. The following chapter is about this.

Now, we explain some **theological concepts** using the OOD terms presented. We do this, as we noticed that some polemics about the *informational* part of *Logos* could get an extra help from such *informational* terms. We present our points in line with Nicaean Creed, without presenting opposing views. For an analysis of polemics, examples of books are "The Philosophy of The Church Fathers" by Harry Wolfson,

---

[16] Spelling 'dialog' for computing, 'dialogue' for humans, per languagetool.org

(Wolfson), "The Spirit of Eastern Christendom" by Jaroslav Pelikan (Pelikan).

We point out that the distinction between *class* and *object* in OOD brings a good support for the distinction between *form* and *object* in Greek thinking. In software, we know where the class is located and its designer; in nature, even if we do not know where it is, we know from the evidence of design that there is a Designer. The *living beings* are special cases, where the *design* is contained in *seeds*, then in every cell, as a CD hard-disk contains *classes*. The designs in seeds correspond to the *expressed thoughts* of the Designer. Starting with the Stoic Zeno, the concept of *Seminal Logos* described the logic contained in seeds, and also by extension the *logical thinking* observed in all the Universe. The Main Seminal Logos dispersed in many *logoi* (logos-es), according to Frank Walton (Bidisham Rectory, UK, 1911) when he explains the Stoics:

> The *Logoi* secured (1) identity through change and (2) development of the individual according to his *class*. The *Logoi* are contained in the *Logos*, and are indeed the multiform manifestation of the *Universal Reason*; and Reason is God. (Walton, 41)

(Note: the above discussion about Zeno is not in the thesis.)

Following are some **theological concepts** using OOD terms:

Case 1 is Paul's text about Lord Jesus' nature, mentioned before; now, we add that the OOD model may help us understand better the difference between a *person* and its *form,* which is like the difference between an *object* and a *class*.

Some people in those times understood the difference; for us, it is an advantage to have handy these *information system* concepts. Paul's text:

> ... Christ Jesus, who, being in the *form* (Gr. morphe) of God, did not consider it robbery to be *equal (Gr. isa) with God*, but made Himself of no reputation, taking the *form* (Gr. morphe) of a bondservant, and coming in the likeness of men. (Phil. 2:5)

Again, *form* means the sum of characteristics, not only 'image' as in usual English. *Forms,* with their *relations*, are part of *logos,* as we know. Modelling this way, the debates about the 'oneness' of the *human* Lord Jesus with God can have a different direction, towards oneness as *form,* not as *person*. Augustine explained oneness by *form*, we presented his thoughts. We add now that with the *information* concepts of *class and objects* we may get a better grasp of the meaning of oneness. We keep in mind though that before incarnation and time, *Logos is God*, per John.

A person has *will,* leading to actions, thus a person has manifestations in time and space, so, a person is not abstract. Lord Jesus in Gethsemani distinguished between His will and the Father's will. However, He said "I and My Father are one" (John 10:30), meaning of same *essence*, per Nicaean Creed.

'*Equal with God'* is an *equality-operator* that compares Jesus' *Form* with God's *Form*, *not* the *human* Jesus (as baby, dying man) as a *person* with the *person* of God.

Case 2 is the *double inheritance*: the person of Christ implements *two forms*, non-exclusive, of God and man, like an object can implement *two classes*, as explained. Such model could help with the debates about the double-being of Jesus. This was the main topic in the early Councils from Nicaea, Constantinople, Ephesus, Chalcedon.

Case 3: at Athens, Paul cites a Greek poet by saying: "we are God's offspring." (Acts17:29) *Offspring* translates *genos* from Greek, also in the previous verse. (Hebr-Gr-Eng Bible). We think that *genos* could be *genus* in English, (Oxford RE) which relates with 'class'. This corresponds to Genessis, that we are made in the image and likeness of God.

The phrase *"we are God's offspring"* contains in Greek another word, besides *genos*: *hyp-arhontes,* that could mean word-by-word *sub-dominion.* It could indicate that a *class* or *genus is a sub-class* from a higher *class or genus.* This looks like *inheritance* in OOD. It could mean that our *genus inherits* from God's *genus.*

As a reminder, *class* and *genus* correspond to *form* in Greek thinking, and *form*s & *their relations* make up a *logos,* the topic of our study. That's why we analyze the *genus* topic.

Note: Cases 4, 5, 6, 7, 8 were not in the Thesis.

Case 4   In the following *text, monogenous* may mean *'unique genus'* (as *class* or *form*):

> We beheld His glory, the glory as of the *only begotten*
> (Gr. *monogenous*) of the Father. (John 1:14*)*

The expression *'only begotten'* attempts to render the meaning of *'monogenous'*, which word-by-word means *unique genus (GR: genos,* per Google Translate*)* which, as explained, is related to the concepts of *form* and *class.* The Son is instantiated as human, but His *genus (form)* is same unique *genus* of the Father.

The same word *monogenous* is used for Isaac, the *second* son of Abraham (the *first* was Ishmael the son of the handmaid). Thus, Isaac is the *'unique genus' (form)* of Abraham, not the *'only son'*. (Hebrews 11:17) [Bible]

Case 5   In John Chapter 1, there are several places where the word *egeneto* is used, translated as 'made' or 'become'. Per Strong, it derives from *ginomai* and means:

> G1096 ginomai ghin'-om-ahee
>
> to cause to be ("*gen*"-erate), i.e. (reflexively) to become (come into being). (Hebr-Gr-Eng Bible)

The meaning "gen"-erate points mainly to making a new entity with a specific *genus (or class, or form)*.

We observe this in verses 2 (egeneto), 10 (egeneto), 12 (genesthai, a variation), 13 (egennethesan) translated THEY-WERE-generatED by (Hebr-Gr-Eng Bible), 14 **(egeneto).**

We point to these verses to show that the concept of *genus*, or *class*, or *form*, can bring a supplementary light when we think about such topics.

Case 6 Another word that has a similar connotation with *class* or *form* is *type*, Gr. *tupos*. It is translated *pattern* in the following text, where God instructs Moses to build the Tabernacle of Meeting:

> He said, "See that you make all things according to the *pattern* (Gr. *tupos*) shown you on the mountain." (Hebrews 8:4)

Here, there is a similarity with the OOD development, where from an abstract *class* (as Greek *form*), the developer instantiates *objects* (ex. from a *Cat class* on hard-disk, some *Cat objects* are generated on display.) Again, *forms & their relations* make up the *system logos*. So, Moses takes the *types* from God's *Logos*, and makes the physical Tabernacle.

Case 7 Another use of *type* (as *class* or *form*): the earthly temple is presented as a *pointer*, Gr. *anti-tupos*, of the true heavenly temple. *Anti-tupos* means a *pointer*, as an arrow directing from a physical entity towards its *type* or pattern.

> For Christ has not entered the holy places made with hands, which are *copies* (Gr. *anti-tupa*, plural of *tupos*) of the true, but into heaven itself, now to appear in the presence of God for us; (Hebrews 9:24)

The similarity with OOD is that we use *pointers* too, from an *object* towards a *class* or another object, to find specific information. In Moses case, the earthly tabernacle points for us towards the heavenly one, thus we learn from the earthly one about the heavenly one.

Case 8 Another use of *type* (as *class* or *form*): Apostle Paul explains that Adam is a '*type* of Him who was to come'; by Adam, we inherit from the same *type*. Form Adam, we inherited the sin and death, from Lord Jesus we inherit the forgiveness of sins and new life:

> Nevertheless, death reigned from Adam to Moses, even over those who had not sinned according to the likeness of the transgression of Adam, who is a *type* of Him who was to come.
>
> But the free gift is not like the offense. For if *by the one man's offense many died*, much more the grace of God and the gift by the grace of the *one Man, Jesus Christ, abounded to many.* (Romans 8:14)

By OOD software, we may understand better how this works: we write a *class* (as a *Cat class*, on hard-disk). The *objects* can be constructed from this *class* (as *Cat objects,* on screen) by calling a *Constructor* function inside the *class*. Also, the objects can be destroyed by calling a *Destructor* function inside the class (a simplified explanation).

Similarly, as we are of Adam's *type* (or *class*), his *punishment* for sin, *death*, was bestowed over us. As we are of the of Christ's *type* (in His *image*), His *payment* for sin was bestowed over us, and we got a new *life*.

Case 9: Several *classes* with their *logical relations* make up a *system logos*, with some useful *external* relations; similarly, we saw how natural and man-made systems, including associations, have the same structure.

We can apply the same structure also in theology: there are many *dialogues* which occur in the Bible, that are like *logical relations* between persons. *Those that relate,* plus their *logical relations* make up, for the duration of the dialogue, a *system logos*. This one can be considered as an entity in itself, as a *Unit,* for the given duration. The dialogues occur between God and men, or between men.

The *Unit* concept directs us to the Hebrew term 'echad', translated with 'one' but could be 'unit'. It is used for *Adam & Eve,* who through their *relations* became a united *family logos*. Also, 'echad' is used in 'Shema Israel' as "*Yahveh Elohi-nu*

Yahveh is one (Hebr. echad)". In this, we could eventually see, like in Adam & Eve case, *persons of Divinity* who through their *relations* make up a *United Deity Logos,* that is united through *Logos*, by dialogue. 'Shema' statement could mean like the statement in John 1:1 *"Logos was with God and Logos was God."*

As said before, even Jewish teachers were thinking that the Deity appearing as a person was a human Presence of the God which heavens of heavens cannot contain, per Solomon. In this view, we wonder if the *two names* in 'Shema' may name this *human Deity* and the *God of heavens*. We could say they are a Unit, through Logos. Philo is not far from such thought.

A thought of the author is that maybe 'echad', taken as numeral 1 instead of 'unit', could be the 'veil' on the face of Israel that keeps them to see the *Logos* that unites Deity, and is Himself God. God is a complex *Unit* (echad) in which *Logos* is of essence (arche).

We wrote all these with deep reverence, because it does not make sense to try to explain God, but also missing what He told us, that *Logos* is God, should not be a choice.

Sure enough, we only add a grain of sand to the great number of discussions, by theology experts, about all the statements we analyzed. In no way we are proposing any definite answer to those debates, we are just giving examples of how information science concepts could eventually help with grasping the informational side of *Logos*.

2. *Coordination of Dialog*

We need a *coordinator* for the *logical relations* (or *dialog*) of a *system* with many *components*, because the relations (internal, external) must happen in a certain order, at specific times, but the components may not know about each other. The *system logos* may be complex and prone to errors without a coordinator.

We can *enhance* here the *system logos* model which has *designs* of components and *their relation*, by adding a *coordinator* for relations. The fundamental model remains the same, but it gets an extra detail. Thus, the *logical relations* between components can be bundled together as a *class*, which with the classes of components make up the *logos* of a system.

We see examples of coordination in human associations:

- The nation of Israel got from God a Law and judges to enforce it. Countries, companies and schools follow that example.
- In the new covenant, God said "I will put My law in their minds, and write it on their hearts." (Jeremiah 31:33) which means that the coordination is *distributed* in the components of the system, rather than being centralized. Everyone knows the Law and enforces it for himself. Thus, it is enforced in the society.
- The Church, as the body of Christ, follows her Head, who is the Coordinator.

Also, in many man-made systems we see coordination, for example an engine has coordination between spark plugs, gas valves and piston movements. We see it also in many natural systems, like the majority of complex animals, which have a central nervous system, brain, coordinating much of their bodies.

As suggested, we could take advantage of *information* science concepts to explain the *informational* part of *logos*. In case of a *system logos* with a *coordinator,* we may take advantage of ideas found in a *software coordination* system.

I designed such a system with *Dialog Coordination* for my Sofware thesis (T. Dumitru, Dialog Coordination). The idea derived from the general (not OOD) *"Coordination Based Design"* by my advisor, Dr. Moshe Krieger (Krieger). The thesis proposed a method for OOD based on *Dialog*, a part of *Logos*, and uses ideas from *John chapter 1*. Observing such a Design Method, we can look in parallel to the natural systems and we could infer that they are designed based on *Logos* too. The process itself of design is also useful to perceive the process of the Creation of God.

I learned from John's statements how to create software systems, as follows:

From John 1.1 *"In the beginning was Logos":*

The design has to start with the desired *logical relations* (*dialog*) between the *User* and the new *System,* as in *"OOD: A Use Case Driven Approach"* by Ivar Jacobson (Jacobson). From these User *logical relations*, we design the rest of the system.

This method corresponds with the statement *"In the beginning was Logos"* because in the beginning of design are *logical relations*, parts of *Logos.*

From John 1.3 *"All things were made through Him (Logos)"*:

From the requirements of the new system, we determine the *User Dialog*. From this, we design the internal *dialogs*, as communications between unknown *components*. Then, we design the internals of these *components*, to make them execute the needed *dialogs*. Thus, the *components* are designed from the requirements for the *User dialog*.

So, we claim that all *components / objects* are made through *Dialog*, like in John 1.3.

From John 1.14 *"Logos became flesh"*:

Internal *Logical relations* (*dialog*) between components should be *coordinated,* otherwise for multiple components the dialog can be prone to errors. I proposed a component called *Coordinator* that receives all dialog messages, orders them based on a pre-designed description, then sends them to destination.

The *Dialog Coordinator* is a *class* implemented as an *object* (a component). We claim that the *Dialog (logical interaction)* can be captured in a *Coordination Object*. All the *system logos* thus becomes a *group of objects*. The *Coordinator is like a head of a body*. This corresponds (I say with reverence) to the text in John *"The Logos became flesh."*

People in John's time understood that *Logos* could be a *'class'* or a *'form'*, but did not know that the *Logos* could become a *body, like a person*. John announces solemnly this incarnation.

If the *components are distributed* on several computers: the Dialog Coordinator *class* is one, but it is implemented in *objects* on each computer. These *objects* maintain an identical status by communication, as when they would be *one object*. We have *'oneness'* of the *Dialog Coordinator class*, but multiple *Dialog Coordinator objects*.

This distributed approach corresponds to the theological concept from Prophet Isaiah about the new Covenant: *"I'll put My Law in their hearts."* The Law as Coordinator is distributed, unlike in the first Covenant, where was written on stones.

3. Error Management Logic

Besides the main design of organisms and of software systems, there is also a design for *Error Corrections* to maintain the systems.

From DNA, an organism generates self-correcting programs, for example the immune systems, which have many kinds of corrections; also, an organism can self-heal and reconstruct partially. In software, engineers add into the design some code that will correct errors of functionality and communications.

Similarly, God pre-designed an error correction process for our wrong doings. Apostle Paul explains in his letter to Romans:

> But now the righteousness of God apart from the law is revealed, … through faith in Jesus Christ, to all and on all who believe. For there is no difference; for all have sinned and fall short of the glory of God, being justified freely by His grace through the redemption that is in Christ Jesus, whom God set forth as a propitiation by His blood, through faith, to demonstrate His righteousness, … that He might be just and the justifier of the one who has faith in Jesus. (Romans 3:21-26)

The Law of God, given through Moses, is a kind of *Logos* with *logical relations* between men and God and between people, *indicating* what is good and what is wrong, but *does not do error correction* once we trespass. The *error correction* is done through Lord Jesus Christ's sacrifice, He suffered 'correction' in our place and *paid the legal debt* of the world towards the requirements of justice. Our part is to realize that the correction was needed because of our sins (Gr. amartian, miss-marks) and to accept the gift made of love. Thus, God maintains the justice and also is graceful by justifying and forgiving us.

A specific error correction mechanism is called *feedback. The concept of feedback* is used for correcting errors in man-made systems. Organisms have by design all kind of error corrections, including feedback based. Societies too implement corrections by feedback for law trespassing.

The feedback is a type of *logical relation,* thus a part of *the logos concept*. A sensor measures the output of a system (e.g., audio amplifier) and gives a *negative signal* to the input, thus correcting the system, if the output (e.g., audio volume) is too high or too low. Without feedbacks, systems can *miss the marked,* expected values.

Also, our Designer implemented an error correction by applying a corrective action on the mankind's Representative who took our *form,* His Son Lord Jesus. Through the *negative feedback* applied on Him, He took away the *miss-marked* values of the mankind. Apostle John says that Jesus Christ is "the Lamb of God who takes away the sins (Gr. amartian, mis-marks) of the world". (John 1:29) There are some other smaller corrective feedbacks, but this ample feedback establishes that mankind is brought back in the parameters of the Law of God, from a broad perspective. Thus, the Designer corrected the mankind as a system, and thus each person, to let us function further. We need to be aware of our miss-marks and need to accept the one-time total correction by feedback on the cross. Also, as we ask our Heavenly Father for our daily bread, we need to ask for our daily forgiveness, and we are forgiven based on the same once-for-all sacrifice of Lord Jesus. Apostle John clarifies this: "If we confess our sins, He is faithful and just to forgive us our sins and to cleanse us from all unrighteousness". (1 John 1:9)

IV. CONCLUSIONS

These things I have spoken to you, that My joy may remain in you, and that your joy may be full.
(John 15:11)

As Lord Jesus spoke to give us His joy, so we did this study to increase our enthusiasm for Him. The centrality of Logos compels us to learn more about Him. We saw how Apostle John brings to front stage His essentiality and equality with God, His fundamental role in Creation, life, light as consciousness, redemption by His sacrifice, maintainer of His new creation - the church. We stand amazed that He loved us till a brutal death, and we are glad He is alive.

We learned that on one side, *Logos* is representing the expressed thinking of a thinker, and for the Cosmos the thinker is Theos. Moreover, we understood that on the other side, everything was made based on *Logos*, which had also the meaning of *designs (forms)* of parts plus their *logical relations*, that make up a *system-logos*. This has a correspondent in the *mind-logos* of the designer; informationally, those two are identical.

These thoughts were developed before Christ. *Logos* was as an intermediary agent connecting God with matter. In Jewish writings, the Word of God, corresponding to *Logos*, connects to people. John declares much more, that *Logos* is God and became flesh. But because Lord Jesus said that He is one with the Father, He was killed for blasphemy. Understanding about *Logos*, as the early church did, is important for us all.

To see how all things are made through *Logos*, we looked at the science domain. Many scientist are missing the light of *Logos*, that shows *purpose* in designs for life, atoms, planetary systems, our mind-system. We looked at natural systems and pointed out their *logos*-like structure, as they are made up of *parts' designs* and their *logical relation*. These derive from their equivalent constructed intentionally in a mind.

In man-made systems, *Logos* plays a central role. We depicted a few projects with *designs of parts* and their *logical relations*, called *system logos*, and said they correlate with similar models in the minds of designers. By expressed thinking, they made projects from their intentional imagination, the *logos* for that case. We can reverse-engineer a system to discover its *logos*. Similarly, we can reverse-engineer natural systems to detect their *logos*.

A special domain is *Information* Science, because *Logos* has an *informational* aspect in the systems' description, besides the personal aspect of a Designer who expresses his thinking. We proposed that we could describe some informational aspects of *Logos* with terms from information Science. By this approach, we can add to the explanation of specific details, as we presented for a few cases.

To sum up, we recall what Lord Jesus said: "All things must be fulfilled which were written in the Law of Moses and the Prophets and the Psalms concerning Me." (Luke 24:44) All the *components* of the Bible, linked by *logical relations*, make up the *Bible-Logos*; this directs to Lord Jesus Christ, the *Logos* Himself. He continues explaining His purpose for us:

Then He said to them, "Thus it is written, and thus it was necessary for the Christ to suffer and to rise from the dead the third day, and that repentance and remission of sins should be preached in His name to all nations, beginning at Jerusalem." (Luke 24:46)

162

He did this because He loved us, as God is Love - in Greek *agape*. *Agape* is unconditional love by respect, it represents a soul-and-mind great relation between two persons, and is a *quality* of *logical relations*. Thus, *agape* exists by *logos*. This discussion leads to another study that I started, mentioned before (T. Dumitru, Edge Observations).

In this context, we could look at the Bible as a description of a dialogue, a sort of *Logos*, between the Lord and men, in which He offers His *agape* for us, with the hope of reaching back *agape* from us. He is asking each of us what He asked Peter: 'Do you *agape* Me?'. The first commandment of ten shows His hope to be loved, but it took His sacrifice to turn our hearts to Him. *Logos* suffered to reach His main goal, the new creation based on *agape* relations- that is the Church, His Bride. We close with a reminder of the Lord's desire before crucifixion:

> With fervent desire I have desired to eat this Passover with you before I suffer; for I say to you, I will no longer eat of it until it is fulfilled in the kingdom of God. (Luke 22:15)

Glory to God!

V. BIBLIOGRAPHY

Aratus. n.d. *Aratus.*
https://en.wikipedia.org/wiki/Aratus#Later_influence.

Aristotle. 1991. *Methapysics.* Amherst, NY: Prometheus Books.

Athanasius. n.d. *Complete Works.* Toronto: e-book.

—. n.d. *Select Works.*
https://biblehub.com/library/athanasius/select_works_and_le
tters_or_athanasius/.

Augustine. n.d. *In_what_manner.*
https://biblehub.com/library/augustine/on_the_holy_trinity/c
hapter_7_in_what_manner_the.htm.

n.d. *Bible.* https://www.biblegateway.com/.

Borchert, Gerald. n.d. *New American Commentary John 1-11.*
Broadman & Holman Publishers.

Boyarin, Daniel. n.d. *"Logos, a Jewish Word: John's Prologue as
Midrash,".*
https://www.academia.edu/36254597/Daniel_Boyarin_Logos_
a_Jewish_Word_John_s_Prologue_as_Midrash_in_Amy_Jill_Le
vine_and_Marc_Zvi_Brettler_eds_The_Jewish_Annotated_Ne
w_Testament_New_York_Oxford_University_Press_2011_546
_549.

n.d. *Britannica.* https://www.britannica.com/topic/logos.

Bush, Russ. 1991. *A Handbook for Christian Philosophy.* Grand Rapids,
Mi: Zondrvan Publishing House.

n.d. *Byzantine_Empire.*
https://en.wikipedia.org/wiki/Byzantine_Empire.

Cavarnos, Constantine. 1975. *The Classical Theory of Relations.*
Belmont: The Institute for Bizantine Studies.

n.d. *Church Fathers.* https://biblehub.com/library/.

Church_Fathers. 2016. *The Complete Ante-Nicene, Nicene and Post-Nicene Collection of Early Church Fathers: Cross-Linked to the Bible.* Toronto: Toronto e-book.

Clark, Gordon. 1972. *Johannine Logos.* Grand Rapids, MI: Baker Book House.

n.d. *Cleanthes_Hymn.*
https://www.academia.edu/15440547/Cleanthes_Hymn_to_Zeus_and_Early_Christian_Literature.

Cleanthes_Stoic. 1921. *The Hymn of Cleanthes.* New York : Macmillan Co., republised by Hardpress Publishing.

Clement. 2020. *Works of Clement.* Omaha, NE: Patristic Publising eBook Amazon.

Clement_of_Alexandria. n.d. *Clement of Alexandria.*
https://www.earlychristianwritings.com/clement.html.

Confessor, Maximus. 2014. *On the Difficulties in the Church Fathers.*
Harvard Colledge, US.

Coxon, A.H. 1999. *Philosophy of Forms.* Assen: Van Gorkum.

Davies, Paul. 2011. *Information and the Nature of Reality.* Cambridge : Cambridge University Press.

Dodd, C. H. 1960. *The Interpratation of the Fourth Gospel.* Cambridge: Cambridge University Press.

Dorn, Douglas Van. 2019. *Christ in the Old Testament.* Watteres of Creation Publishing.

Drozdek, Adam. 2018. *Greek Philosophers as Theologians.* New York: Ashgate Publishing.

Dumitru, Cristian. 2000. *Biblical Architecture.* Bucharest: Evangelical Romanian Society.

Dumitru, Teodor. n.d. *Daniel* . https://teostory.files.wordpress.com/2022/01/seventy_all.big_.leters.miki_-1.pdf.

—. 2000. *Dialog Coordination.* https://www.collectionscanada.gc.ca/obj/s4/f2/dsk1/tape4/PQDD_0016/MQ57110.pdf.

—. n.d. *Edge Observations.* https://teostory.wordpress.com/jos-wedding/.

—. n.d. *Isaiah* . https://teostory.wordpress.com/209-2/.

—. n.d. *Logos as Expressed Thinking.* San Diego: Teodor Dumitru self publishing on Kindle Direct Publishing.

n.d. *Encyclopedia Britanica.* https://pressbooks.bccampus.ca/humanbiology053/chapter/5-6-protein-synthesis/#:~:text=This%20process%20is%20called%20protein,of%20messenger%20RNA%20(mRNA).

Epimenides. n.d. *Epimenides.* https://en.wikipedia.org/wiki/Epimenides.

Eusebius. n.d. *Church History.* https://www.ccel.org/ccel/schaff/npnf201.iii.vi.ii.html.

—. 1993. *History of Christianity.* Oxford, UK: Oxford University Press.

Evans, Craig. n.d. *Word and Glory.* Journal for the Studies of the New Testament Series 89.

Farrar, Richard. 2001. *Plato and Object Oriented Programming.* Accessed 2010. https://www.richardfarrar.com/plato-and-object-oriented-programming/.

n.d. *Fathers Origen.* https://www.newadvent.org/cathen/11306b.htm.

Floridi, Luciano. n.d. *Informational Realism.* https://www.academia.edu/9330560/Informational_Realism .

Gitt, Werner. 2006. *"In the beginning was information".* Green Forest: First Master Books Printing.

n.d. *Gutenberg Sophist.* https://www.gutenberg.org/files/1735/1735-h/1735-h.htm.

n.d. *Hebr-Gr-Eng Bible.* scripture4all.org.

Heidegger, Martin. 2019. *Heraclitus.* London: Bloomsbury Publishing.

—. 2003. *Plato's Sophist.* Bloomington: Indiana University Press.

Hillar, Marian. n.d. *IEP-Philo.* https://iep.utm.edu/philo/.

n.d. *Irreducible Complexity.* https://carm.org/creation-evolution/what-is-irreducible-complexity/.

Jacobson, Ivar. 1992. *Object-Oriented Software Engineering: A Use Case Driven Approach.* Boston: Addison-Wesley.

Justin. n.d. *Dialogue with Tripho .* https://biblehub.com/library/justin/dialogue_of_justin_philosopher_and_martyr_with_trypho/index.html.

Justin-the-Martyr. 2014. *Writings of Justin the Martyr.* Veritas Splendor Publications.

Keller, Timothy. 1950. *The Reason for God.* New York: Penguin Group.

Kostenberger, Andreas. n.d. *John - Baker Exegetical Commentary.* grand Rapids, MI: Baker Academic.

Krieger, Moshe. 1998. *Coordination Based Design.* ObjectTime Workshop on Research in Real-Time OOM.

Kuhlewind, Georg. 2014. *The Logos Structure of the World* . Lindisfarne Press.

Ladd, George. n.d. *A Theology of the New Testament.* Grand Rapids, MI: William Eerdmans Publishing Co.

Laertius, Diogenes. n.d. *Lives of the Eminent Philosophers.* Oxford: Oxford University Press - eBook Amazon.

Lange, John. n.d. *Commentary on the Holly Scriptures / John-Acts.* Grand Rapids, MI: Zondervan Publishing House.

Law, Timothy Michael. 2013. *The Septuagint in the New Testament.* https://academic.oup.com/book/6258/chapter-abstract/149903383.

McArthur, John. 2017. *The Deity of Christ.* Chicago: Moody Publishers.

McFarland, Ian. 2019. .*The Word Made Flesh.* Louisville: Westminster John Knox Press.

MESKOS, GEORGE. n.d. *Logos in Modern Physics.* https://www.academia.edu/12881725/THE_NOTION_OF_LOGOS_FROM_HERACLITUS_TO_MODERN_PHYSICS?email_work_card=view-paper.

Nicene_Creed. n.d. https://www.earlychurchtexts.com/public/nicene_creed.htm.

n.d. *Nobel Prize 2023.* https://www.theguardian.com/science/2023/sep/14/breakthrough-prize-winners-2023-science.

Nunez, Paul. 2016. *The Science of Consciousness.* Amherst: Prometheus Books.

n.d. *Origen on John.* https://www.newadvent.org/fathers/101501.htm.

Origen. n.d. *Works.* eBook Amazon.

Owen, John. n.d. *Appearances of the Son of God under the Old Testament.* Watteres of Creation Publishing.

n.d. *Oxford RE.*
https://oxfordre.com/classics/display/10.1093/acrefore/97801
99381135.001.0001/acrefore-9780199381135-e-2818#.

Para, Sean. 2018. *Platonism, Object Oriented Programming.*
https://medium.com/@spara77/platonism-object-oriented-
programming-and-the-persistence-of-philosophical-traditions-
in-western-b10fbbb387e0.

n.d. *Parmenides.* https://www.austincc.edu/adechene/Parmenides.

Patrick Grim, Daniel Singer. 2020. *Computational Philosophy.*
https://plato.stanford.edu/entries/computational-philosophy/
.

Patrick, T. 2013. *The Fragments of Heraclitus.* Digireads Publishing,
eBook Amazon.

Pelikan, Jaroslav. 1974. *The Spirit of Eastern Christendom.* University of
Chicago Press.

n.d. *Philo of Alexandria.* https://sblhs2.com/2018/03/01/philo-of-
alexandria/.

Philo. 2021. *The Works of Philo.* Peabody: Hendrickson Publishers.

n.d. *Plato Parmenides.*
http://www.perseus.tufts.edu/hopper/text?doc=Perseus%3At
ext%3A1999.01.0174%3Atext%3DParm.%3Asection%3D135a.

Plato. 1997. *Plato Complete Works.* Indianapolis: Hacket Publishing.

n.d. *Plato, Sophist.*
http://www.perseus.tufts.edu/hopper/text?doc=Perseus%3At
ext%3A1999.01.0172%3Atext%3DSoph.%3Asection%3D251d.

2007. *Presocratic Philosophy.*
https://plato.stanford.edu/entries/presocratics/.

n.d. *Republic.*
http://www.faculty.umb.edu/michael_lafargue/104/204/plato
/readings/plato-txt-5-05.htm.

Reymond, Robert. n.d. *John, Beloved Disciple* .

Rovelli, Carlo. 2017. *Reality is Not What it Seems.* New York: Penguin
Random House.

Sallis, John. 1975. *Being and Logos.* Bloomington: Indiana University.

Schaff, Philip. n.d. *Excursus on the Word Homousios.*
https://biblehub.com/library/schaff/the_seven_ecumenical_c
ouncils/excursus_on_the_word_homousios.htm.

Schnelle, Udo. n.d. *Antidocetic Christology.* Minneapolis: Fortress
Press.

Schrock, Terrill. 2017. *The Logos in Language and Religion.*
https://www.academia.edu/79251336/The_Logos_in_Languag
e_and_Religion.

n.d. *Sophist.*
http://www.perseus.tufts.edu/hopper/text?doc=Perseus%3At
ext%3A1999.01.0172%3Atext%3DSoph.%3Asection%3D260a.

n.d. *Stanford_Philo.* https://plato.stanford.edu/entries/philo/.

n.d. *Stoicism Debate.* https://modernstoicism.com/the-debate-do-you-
need-god-to-be-a-stoic/.

1993. *The Works of Philo Judaeus.*
http://www.earlychristianwritings.com/yonge/.

Thomas, Brian. n.d. *Creation.* https://creation.com/cell-systems.

n.d. *Timaeus.*
https://www.perseus.tufts.edu/hopper/text?doc=Perseus%3At
ext%3A1999.01.0179%3Atext%3DTim.%3Asection%3D38c.

Vennaro, Nick. n.d. *plato-oo-design.*
https://www.vennaro.com/blog/plato-oo-design-and-why-you-should-read-widely.

Walton, Frank. 1911. "Development of Logos Doctrine ." Bristol: John Wright and Sons Ltd.

n.d. *Wisdom of Solomon.* https://ebible.org/pdf/eng-web/eng-web_WIS.pdf.

Wolfson, Harry. 1956. *The Philosophy of the Church Fathers. Vol 1.* Harvard University Press .

Yegge, John Gerard. 2014. *A Historical Analysis of the Relationship of Faith and Science and its Significance within Education.* https://scholarworks.waldenu.edu/cgi/viewcontent.cgi?article=1081&context=dissertations.

Sources Consulted

Augustine. 1993. *The City of God.* Random House, NY

Barnard, L. W. (1971). *The Logos Theology of St Justin Martyr.* The Downside Review, 89(295), 132–141. https://doi.org/10.1177/001258067108929502

Beeke & Smalley. 2019. *Reformed Systematic Theology.* Wheaton: Crossway

Church Fathers. *2016. The Complete Works of Church Fathers.* Toronto: e-book

Clement of Alexandria Writings.
https://www.earlychristianwritings.com/clement.html#google_vignette

Crossant, John. 1998. *The Birth of Christianity.* New York: HarperCollins Publishers

David Horton. 2006. *The Portable Seminary*. Bethany House Publishers, Bloomington, MN

Duchesne, Louis. 2017. Early History of Christian Church. E-book, Amazon

Earle Cairns. 1954. *Christianity through the Centuries*. Zondervan Publishing House, Grand Rapids, Mi

Early Christian Writings. https://www.earlychristianwritings.com/tixeront/section1-5.html#clement

Grudem, Wayne. 1994. *Systematic Theology.* Grand Rapids: Zondervan

Hayes, Jerry. 2015. *Godhead Theology.* Texas City: Seventh Millenium Publications

Henry, Mathew. 1997. *Commentary on the Whole Bible.* Nashville: Thomas Nelson, Inc.

Jonathan Hill. 2006. *History of Christianity*. Lion Publishing, Oxford, UK

Justin-the-Martyr. 2014. *Writings of Justin the Martyr.* Veritas Splendor Publications

Sproul, R.C. 1984. *Classical Apologetics.* Grand Rapids: Zondervan Co.

Made in the USA
Monee, IL
03 May 2024

57748990R00098